AF470928

# The World of
# WILLIAM WICKHAM

*The biography and photography
of a remarkable Victorian*

*by Kenneth Ward*

*with many original photographs
dating back to the 19th century*

*Published by Ian Harrap at
THE PALLANT PRESS
HAVANT: HANTS*

First published in Great Britain 1981
by The Pallant Press, Havant, Hants





ISBN 095071410 0

Printed in Great Britain by Adlard & Son Ltd, Bartholomew Press, Dorking

# CONTENTS


1. Introduction   1
2. William Arthur Wickham: Trowbridge to Wigan — 1849—1879   3
3. The Wigan of Mr Wickham   13
4. The Building Vicar   16
5. Photography and Mr Wickham   29
6. The Lantern Shows   38
7. Marriage and Family Background   48
8. Honeymoon in Switzerland: 1892   53
9. Coal-mining and the Coal Strikes   60
10. The St. Andrew's Parish Magazine   72
11. Family Life at Wigan   82
12. Duties and Diversions   91
13. Wigan to Ampton   99
14. Life at Ampton   106

*ACKNOWLEDGEMENTS*

My grateful thanks are due especially to Miss Cicely Wickham, Dr. Monica Wickham and Miss Caroline Wickham for their enthusiastic encouragement; and for their patient forbearance during the many hours of mind-racking recollection. Also, for the provision of so much invaluable material.

And, among others, my thanks to Mr. Wilfred Ashurst, on behalf of St. Andrew's Church, Wigan, whose energies led me up so many 'fruitful avenues'; to Mr. R. E. Lassam, Curator, The Fox Talbot Museum, for photographic information; to the Rev. Richard Norburn, Rector of Ampton; to Mr. D. Anderson, The Quaker House Colliery Co. Ltd., Billinge; to Mr. and Mrs. C. P. Seyd; to the staff of the Wigan, and Bury St. Edmunds Record Offices; to the City of London Mission; and to the Department of Civil and Mechanical Engineering, The Science Museum, London.

Kenneth C. Ward

Meonstoke
April 1980

*LIST OF ILLUSTRATIONS*

*Page*

6 *Netley Abbey, near Southampton*
6 *'Killiechassie' Drawing Room, Perthshire*
7 *Romsey Abbey interior*
8 *Picture boat on the Leeds—Liverpool Canal; Wigan, 1891*
8 *Haughmond Chapter-House, c.1150*
9 *Surveying team, putting direction lines on a pit roadway*
9 *Sandringham Church. A sketch by William Wickham*
20 *St. Andrew's Church, Wigan; East Aspect, 1882*
20 *Interior view of St. Andrew's Church*
21 *St. Andrew's Schools, Wigan*
21 *Angel playing a stringed instrument; pew carving in choir stalls, 1892*
21 *The Litany Desk*
22 *Advent Hunstone carving*
22 *The Eagle Lectern*
22 *Misericord in choir stalls*
23 *St. Cecilia at organ with little blower; pew end carving*
23 *Reverse of St. Cecilia pew-end carving*
23 *Detail of choir-stall pew, with poppy-head*
23 *David playing his harp; pew-end carving*
32 *Collier waiting; Wigan, 1891*
32 *Anxious faces, interested faces; taken at St. Andrew's Soup Kitchen, 1893*
33 *Collier 'keawring' (squatting), 1891*
34 *Old lady in doorway, 1891*
35 *Cruachan Burn, pre-1884*
35 *Yacht at Oban, pre-1884*
41 *Steering gear; taken near Wigan, 1891*
41 *The fish hawker; Wigan, 1891*
42 *Good news or bad?; receiving the Boat Examiner's report, 1891*
42 *Elderly parishioner in bed; Wigan, 1891*
43 *Christmastide; City of London Mission representative distributing gifts to boat children, 1891*
43 *The bread oven; Wigan, 1891*
44 *Wash-day in the alley; back-to-back cottages in the parish, 1891*
44 *St. Andrew's Mothers' Meeting; 1891*

55 *Chapel and Fusshorner*
55 *Sunlight and shade; village scene*
55 *The ice table; the Aletsch Glacier*
56 *Helping hand; Tony, the guide, assists Mrs. Wickham*
57 *Roped together; Mr. and Mrs. Wickham with guide. Ascent of the Beichgrat (10,300 ft)*
57 *Cautiously does it; Mrs. Wickham feeling for a foothold*
58 *Guide at Ravine*
58 *On the Aletsch Glacier*
58 *Baggage transport at the hotel*
64 *Miner setting a prop*
64 *St. Andrew's Soup Kitchen; Mr. Haworth serving. The 1893 Coal Strike*
65 *Drawer pushing tub*
65 *Collier under-cutting and boy drilling*
66 *St. Andrew's Soup Kitchen, 1893, Mr. Wickham serving*
67 *Collier entering cage; Douglas Bank Colliery, 1891*
67 *Cage arriving at bottom, 1891*
67 *Collier washing in kitchen, 1891*
67 *Collier taking his ease, 1891*
85 *The Vicarage Dining Room*
85 *The Vicarage Drawing Room*
86 *Bernard on rug, 1894*
86 *Bernard with foxglove*
86 *Bernard in Christ's Hospital uniform, 1907*
86 *Lt. Bernard Wickham, M.C., 1916*
87 *All five at the tent*
87 *Bernard and Myrtle*
87 *Myrtle asleep in pram*
88 *Bernard and Myrtle on rug*
88 *Cicely in Vicarage doorway, 1907*
88 *Mrs. Martha Peck*
97 *A selection of Mr. Wickham's literary works*
97 *Page from programme for a St. Andrew's sale of work*
101 *Dressed in their best; miners' women with 'snap' — baskets and tea urns, 1891*
102 *Pay-day crowd*
102 *Pit-brow lasses*
103 *Loosening and 'filling' coal, after blowing the face, 1891*
103 *Wigan; rag-and-bone man, 1891*
107 *Ampton Church; Henry Calthorpe Memorial*
107 *Ampton Church; Dorothy Calthorpe Memorial*
111 *Photography for 'Some notes on Chapter Houses'*
112 *Photography in the West Country*

*REFERENCES*

My acknowledgements and thanks are due for information obtained from the following sources:

1.   'This is Your Church' (History of St. Andrew's Church, Wigan) (1962).
2.   'Twixt Liverpool and Leeds': a Wigan Archive Teaching unit (compiled by P. H. Carey. 1978).
3.   'The History and Development of the Wigan Coalfield' (Wigan Metropolitan Borough Museums Service).
4.   'Victorian Lancashire' by S. P. Bell (ed.) (David Charles, 1974).
5.   'Commercial Review of Leading Firms in Important Towns: Wigan, 1895.'
6.   'Historical Geography of Wigan: A Methodological Study' (J. M. Hayton. 1967–1971).
7.   'The Wigan Borough Guide, 1971.'
8.   'Changes in the Location of Population and Industry in Wigan, from 1850 to 1968' (Doreen Croghan, November 1968).
9.   'Housing and Social Structures in mid-Victorian Wigan and St. Helens' (J. T. Jackson, 1977).
10.   The Victoria County History of Lancashire.
11.   Worrell's Directory of Wigan (1881).
12.   The Wigan Almanac (1893).
13.   'LIFE' Library of Photography (Time Life International).
14.   'The Wigan Coalfield Exhibition Workbook' (H. Airey, Wigan Archives Education Officer).
15.   'My Hometown — Wigan' (Florence Talbot), Article in 'Lancs. Evening Post and Chronicle', September 27th, 1976.

*Note on the photographs.* The best reproductions are those made from Mr. Wickham's original glass plate negatives (O.G.P.). The lantern slides (L.S.) lack contrast; and some carry much irremovable 'dirt' adhering to the emulsion, through long exposure to air and damp, without protective cover (reproducing on my negatives). The album prints (A.P.) are better, considering their age (about 100 years old), and made copy negative production easier.

K.W.

*Photographs of the family.* Family photographs 'tail off' in 1907, the year in which Mr. Wickham seems to have launched himself into the research and production of papers on church architecture and similar subjects. There are no good, reproducible photographs of either Monica or Caroline in their childhood, nor of Mrs. Wickham or the family together.

# Chapter 1


## *INTRODUCTION*

It all began when, like the three wise men bearing gifts, three elderly ladies from a neighbouring village came into my pharmacy in Droxford, each bearing with careful tread a black box about 10 in. × 4 in. × 4 in. with obviously weighty contents. They were the three surviving daughters of the family of the Rev. W. A. Wickham, and customers of mine.

"Mr. Ward", said Dr. Monica Wickham, "this is the remaining part of our father's collection of glass plate photographs; we have sent the rest back to Wigan, where we feel they belong. When we are dead, these will only be thrown out. We thought that, with your interest in photography, you were the most suitable person to have them."

I demurred, suggesting that they be sent to some particular archives or other, but the ladies pressed me to accept them. I took them home and, wonderingly, began to investigate the contents of the boxes.

Some were positive lantern slides; the remainder, about 300, were negative plates. Almost all were in individual envelopes, tabulated with a reference number; many were titled and some dated. Intrigued, I pulled out plates at random. Some had spoiled due to age and storage; some were not of good quality; but many were in very good condition and, by the light of my enlarger, appeared to be exceptionally remarkable photographs. Dates on the envelopes went from 1882 to 1915.

There were photographs of young children (his family); people on mountainous, snowy slopes in rather incongruous attire (his honeymoon photographs, taken in 1892 in Switzerland, I found out); street hawkers; miners; church photographs; house interiors; general scenes; a fascinating and varied collection.

Later, I selected a few and, having printed them reasonably well, made greetings cards of them and sent them to family and friends.

Time passed. I moved to Meonstoke, which had an old, leaky, corrugated-iron and timber hut for a village hall — a construction fast becoming unfit for use. An enthusiastic band of people had formed a committee with a view to raising enough money to build a new village hall. I wondered: how about a photographic exhibition, using the material on the glass plates?

I went to see the Misses Wickham, and put the idea to them. They were enthusiastic, and promised to write to a friend in Wigan to find out if the remainder of the collection could be borrowed from there. The answer was 'yes'.

I went to Wigan and came back with more black boxes, lots of archive material, and good and bad news. The glass plates sent there had deteriorated, due to damp and fungal action; almost all were ruined. Fortunately, the collection included about 100 positive lantern slides, made from the original negatives by Mr. Wickham. These had suffered less damage, had been retrieved by a church-warden, and the cover glasses re-bound. I could make new negatives from the best of them — about 70 in all.

The three ladies began to turn out the contents of drawers and cupboards, producing letters, press cuttings, parish magazines, note-books, piles of loose prints, and two complete photograph albums containing nearly 250 prints taken before 1885.

I went to work. The next six months seemed to be all dark-room work, interspersed with round-the-table talks during which many forgotten memories were rekindled by the photographs I had reproduced. I hastily scribbled notes as the Misses Wickham reminisced pleasurably and excitedly.

Five days before E-day, the material was ready: about 250 enlargements accompanied by much background matter occupying the space of 40 large Daler boards. Press and radio publicity spread the news of the Exhibition and during the three days many people came from all over Hampshire.

The Science Museum in London sent a representative to see the photographs Mr. Wickham had taken down a coal-mine in 1891 (and subsequently ordered many for their records); the Mayor of Romsey came and ordered two sets of the Romsey Abbey photographs taken in 1869 (one set for presentation to Earl Mountbatten, sadly murdered the very next day); other people, particularly archivists, showed interest; and the New Village Hall Fund profited.

The first of the Reverend William Arthur Wickham's works was coming to light.

Chapter 2


## *WILLIAM ARTHUR WICKHAM: TROWBRIDGE TO WIGAN — 1849 to 1879*

William Arthur Wickham, born in 1849, was the eldest of the five children of William Wickham, grocer, of Trowbridge, Wiltshire, and Emma Sophia Wickham. Two brothers and two sisters followed.

Late in life, he wrote of his father as "very much a Saint, being near to God continually, so far as we could tell...On Sunday, he went to Sunday School to take a class of young men; then to Morning Prayer, Litany, and once a month, Holy Communion. A short rest after luncheon, then again to afternoon Sunday School. Then, often, he would visit some sick or poor people and read and pray with them. Then to Evening Service followed by supper and bed. That was his rest-day."

William Wickham Senior, served devotedly as churchwarden at the parish church and was presented with a silver snuffbox as a testimonial. When he died, aged 58, in 1865 it threw a great burden on his widow, Emma, who prior to her marriage to him had to 'mother' half-a-dozen younger brothers and sisters after her own mother's death. Now here she was with five children aged from 8 to 16 years.

William Wickham's will was a splendid quill-written parchment about a metre square. His very first consideration was a small legacy to the Church Missionary Society. The income from the residue, left to his widow, was not great. Some help came from relatives and it is believed that her family, the Rummings, helped particularly in the matter of the education of the children.

Emma Wickham's father was a farmer at Wingfield, near Trowbridge; and young William remembered him as "a kind, apple-faced old man who lived to be over 80 and died of paralysis". Despite hard times, Emma Wickham lived to almost 90, spending her later years with one of her sons, Martyn, who also entered the Church.

In his brief autobiographical notes, jotted down in his 70s, the Rev. Wickham wrote of his grandfather's forbears as farmers in

Wiltshire: also of one, a wine merchant in London, who had black servants. He recalled his pleasant times at relatives' farms: riding to Figheldean in his Uncle William's gig; going to Salisbury market with him and bringing back salmon and other delicacies... "they always had a nice table, and I was made to behave myself and to eat properly".

Of his mother he wrote "She was nice-looking and a good house-wife — the kindest and best of mothers, and of wives. She was deeply religious, growing more so as she aged. I cannot remember that she had any amusements beyond her house, family, and garden. She did her best to make us good Christians. I think we clung more to her than to our father...."

Trowle Farm was, undoubtedly, young William's favourite place; he often went there, to his uncle Tom's... "I enjoyed the life there, but it was cold getting between the sheets at night. I ate many apples, pears, mulberries and blackberries. I used to borrow my uncle's gun (powder horn and shot pouch) and go shooting, my Aunts being in a fearful state of alarm, until I got back again."

William's first school was a small private school run by two sisters, the Misses Rolls, and their brother Ambrose. Here, he learned to write and to draw and studied music... "but, musically, I did not get on. I was sent into the front parlour to practise but a good proportion of the time was spent looking at fossils, ores, and other curiosities there...."

When about 10 years old, he was sent to the newly opened Trowbridge Grammar School. He recalled the first Master, the Rev. Gawn, who was brought back dead one day after bursting a blood vessel whilst out riding... "I once saw him trying to drown a dog... I loved him more after he was dead than I did before..."

His successor, the Rev. C. B. Wardale, gave young William Wickham his only flogging... "He flogged me in real earnest, taking off his gown and dragging me down the room and back again. I had resented being put across his knee for a spanking, and I believe I kicked him. But I didn't deserve the flogging..."

He was taught Latin by the second master, the Rev. H Bedingfield... "He used to take infinite pains with his sermons, copying them out in a kind of copper-plate writing and reading them with such violent action of his rather tubby little head as makes one headachy to think of..."

Soon after his father's death, William left school. He had been confirmed a little earlier. "My confirmation was the greatest blessing..." He went as junior teacher in a private school at Highgate, North London, and stayed there for two years, recalling them as "not unhappy years".

Subsequently, he travelled about doing private tutoring. No record remains of this part of his life other than the photographs taken by him. Then, in 1873, he entered Lichfield Theological College and was later ordained. His first post was as Curate to a church in the colliery village of Talke-o-the-Hill, in Staffordshire.

It is likely that he had his first practical experience of photography in 1869, with someone owning one of the 'View' cameras of that period, for we have nine photographs of Hampshire 'landmarks', captioned in his hand-writing, with some dated to the day. That year his photograph had been taken by a Southampton professional photographer, so perhaps a friendship had grown up between them — or Mr. Wickham had been engaged as tutor and had become interested in this new art form.

By 1884, Mr. Wickham had done a considerable amount of photography for, in that year, he presented to his bride-to-be an album of prints covering his travels, dating the album and endorsing it "To Clara" (Miss Clara Peck). In this album and a further contemporary one are some 240 photographs; many are of churches, abbeys, chapter houses, cathedrals, and associated architectural detail. Interspersed with these, as though incidental to his main interests, are scenes or subjects that 'caught his eye': the old cross at Bovey Tracey, a yacht at Oban, the Butter Walk at Dartmouth, and some very fine house interiors at 'Killiechassie', which was perhaps a retreat house.

Bearing in mind the technical problems associated with early photography and photographic processing, these photographs, in composition, detail and reproductive quality, are clearly indicative of, to say the least, a very competent student. In my dark-room, working from the original materials, I had constantly to re-convince myself that I was reproducing photographs nearly 100 years old.

At Talke-o-the-Hill, Mr. Wickham found himself in a parish with a rapidly expanding population and an inadequate and uncomfortable church. Land had been given for a site for a new church; and, of the estimated £4,000 required, £650 had been promised together with all the stone needed. On December 30th, 1876 the Rev. Wickham's first appeal letter went out, and by 1878 the foundation stone had been laid. Mr. Wickham was gaining experience that was to prove of great value later.

In the summer of that year he went on holiday to Lugano. At that time he was expecting the definite offer of another appointment. Instead came a letter from Canon Bridgeman, Rector of Wigan, offering him St. Andrew's. Mr. Wickham wrote for further details. In the meantime the offer he had been expecting arrived, delayed by a simple act of forgetfulness. Then came a further letter from

*Netley Abbey, near Southampton. Wet-plate photography, August 1869 (captioned and dated by Mr. Wickham. (A.P.)*

*'Killiechassie' Drawing Room, Perthshire. Dry-plate photography, probably 1883 (A.P.)*

'Romsey Abbey interior.' Wet-plate photography — probable exposure time 30 minutes or more. (A.P.)

*'Picture boat on the Leeds—Liverpool Canal': Wigan, 1891. (L.S.)*

*'Haughmond Chapter-House', c. 1150 (Order of Austin or Black Canons): Norman Style. (A.P.)*

Surveying team, putting direction lines on a pit roadway.

'Sandringham Church.' Signed and dated sketch, by Mr. Wickham, Easter, 1871.

Wigan, so he wrote to both patrons asking for time to consider the position.

After his holiday he contacted Canon Bridgeman and went to Wigan. He wrote later of the uninviting look of the place and the immensity of the task before him if he accepted the living. Then he went away to a quiet place in Derbyshire to get the advice of a trusted friend.

In his farewell letter to the parishioners of St. Andrew's, 38 years later, he wrote, "It was very difficult to see the path of duty. I never prayed more earnestly in my life, but at last the way was made clear — and I accepted St. Andrew's with my eyes open, but without a misgiving. To be able to feel sure that God has sent one to a place is in itself a Benediction."

He arrived in Wigan on November 2nd, 1878, and read himself in at the Martland Bridge School-cum-Church on the following day.

In February 1879, at the annual St. Andrew's congregational tea-party, reviewing the situation he had taken over, Mr. Wickham dealt at length with the circumstances surrounding his decision. He drew a parallel between the relationship of pastor and parish as between bridegroom and bride. Speaking frankly, yet amusingly, he made clear his expecations of his parishioners.

The local press reported the new Vicar's address verbatim; and one reads... "It was the custom, when a Bishop was consecrated, to present him with a ring to remind him that he was married to his diocese. Now a Bishop is only a parish priest on a large scale... and therefore there would be no impropriety in the newly-appointed vicar of a parish wearing an espousal ring; or, at any rate, if he does without a ring, in regarding his parish as his bride.

"It pleases me, dear people, to allow thus much play to my imagination. I regard St. Andrew's as my bonnie bride, and there is one advantage in a marriage of that sort that, whereas in ordinary wedlock the husband has to support that wife, in this case I shall expect my parish to support me.

"I once heard a story of a man who was being married, and the point in the service was reached at which he was asked 'Wilt thou, John, have this Jane, etc?' The bridegroom paused for a minute, as if in deep thought, and then gave the answer 'Eh, maister, that aw will, though aw'd reyther hev ho sister'.

"Now there is this difference between that man and myself — that I might have had 'ho sister', had I so chosen, for she was offered to me at the same time; and I may inform you that she was much richer and, if you won't be offended, I will add far more comely than you are.

"When I go my rounds amongst you, I continually hear the

expression 'We are a very poor parish'; and, taking into consideration the absence of church and vicarage, the perpetual fogs and smoke, the constant floods, the long rows of cottages, the roads which remind one more of swamp tracks rather than of streets of an ancient borough — taking all these things into consideration, no-one will accuse you of being too handsome.

"Well, if you promise to keep the secret, I will tell you that it was your very poverty and lack of beauty which drew my heart-strings towards you. I made the choice I did because I thought if I chose you I could not be fairly blamed for 'marrying for money' or for being 'caught by a pretty face'.

"And now, dear friends, arises the question how our married life will be lived out . . .

". . . A friend of mine earnestly impressed upon me, some time ago, the necessity of at once 'getting to the bottom of my parish', and he selfishly suggested that the quickest way would be for me to take him down a coal-pit, which he much wished to see.

"In a weak moment, I consented, and I will tell you the result. A sharp-eyed parishioner watched us as we got out of the cage at the bottom; and, when he came to the surface, he made these remarks to a friend . . . 'Yar minister's bin down pit today. Eh! au were fain. Ha were fair moidered: awst think there's no pits where ha coom fra.' [Your Vicar has been down the pit, today. Oh! I was pleased. He was very worried: I would think there are no pits where he comes from.]

"That was what they thought of me at the bottom of my parish! . . . Mutual understanding is the stepping-stone to mutual love and mutual patience. That is the grand secret of a quiet married life. The parish and the pastor each have need of patience. If either lack this grace, the other leads a weary life. The parish has a right to expect from a pastor that his best strength, his best thought, and his best energies shall be spent in her service.

"And the pastor has no less a right to expect from his parish responsive earnestness, and an ever-growing confidence. I dare to hope, dear people, at the commencement of my ministry amongst you, not that we shall be without troubles — for that would be both unnatural and unhealthy — but that grace may be given to me to be faithful to your best interests; and to you to be obedient to the truth which I deliver . . ."

From this point, through the sheets of the soon-to-be-launched parish magazine, through reports in the local press, through observations and appreciations of people who were to get to know him and to work for him — both in the parish and outside it — we get a clear picture of the man.

He had a great capacity for learning, with the practical application to go with it. He was a man of tremendous energy, purposefully directed; a man of strong views and unflinching principles from which he could not be moved; a man of clear-minded vision; a man of great faith. And with it all, a fine sense of humour that breaks through the grim seriousness of his 38 years of planning, fund-raising, evangelising, succouring, sympathising, creating, and chastising fearlessly on occasion.

Not for nothing has Mr. Wickham gone down in the St. Andrew's parish records as the 'Building Vicar'. The parish magazine sheets for 30 of those 38 years, other content apart, are continuing statements of indebtedness to be redeemed. A great parish machinery — religious, social service, educational and recreational — was built on faith.

The miracle of it all was that he still found so much time to do so much more in so many other ways, as shall be revealed.

Chapter 3

## *THE WIGAN OF MR. WICKHAM*

Mr. Wickham had good cause to prefer 'ho sister' appointment, for Wigan was not a pleasant place in which to live — least of all the area near to the river and the canal.

The Victoria County History of Lancashire, at the turn of the 19th century, probably gave an accurate description of the borough as it was throughout his ministry at St. Andrew's. It said of the West Derby Hundred..."the whole district is thickly populated, the industrial town of Wigan occupying the greater part of its township, whilst its collieries, factories, etc., fill the atmosphere with smoke... the southwesterly part of the township lies very low, and is almost always flooded, the result of frequent subsidencies of the ground".

And much was unchanged when a parishioner, Florence Talbot, spent her childhood there two decades later. The long rows of mean little cottages, each with its small backyard, outside closet, and tin bath on the wall, were still there. So was the atmosphere, thick with smoke and smuts from the belching chimneys. One of her favourite recollections was of the day when an inquisitive window-cleaner rubbed away at a plate on the wall of her house to reveal, to her childish delight, the name of the street in which she lived.

It had been Henry III who, granting the town its first charter, bestowed remarkable rights on the church there — rights which, when finally relinquished in the 19th century, provide a thread in the pattern of this story.

In medieval times, the town had been built around the 12th century church and the central market place. Wigan was very much self-supporting, including the making of woollens, pottery, leather-work, brass, iron and pewter-work; and with both outcrop and shallow-pit coal mining on a small scale. The special 'cannel' coal of Wigan, high in gas content, was to become highly-prized.

The 17th century saw the establishment of ironworks on a small scale, the growth of pewtering and the beginning of clock-making, as well as the commercialisation of the collieries. But the development of the canals and, later, the coming of the railways were the two factors that changed the industrial face of Wigan, providing cheap transportation for bulk materials.

A canal parallel to the River Douglas had been made in 1727; this was extended to Liverpool in 1772. Later it became a part of the great Leeds—Liverpool Canal, opened in 1816. By 1880 the canal system extended to all parts of Lancashire and to the West Riding of Yorkshire. Linking up with other canal systems, it enabled raw materials and finished goods to be taken to many parts of England.

In 1831 the railways came to Wigan, linking the town first with Liverpool and Manchester and later with extensions elsewhere.

Over this period, great technical developments in coal mining and the establishment of large ironworks hastened industrial growth and new developments in the area. A look at the Wigan Directory, around the time of settling-in of Mr. Wickham as Vicar of Wigan St. Andrew's, reveals the nature of the changes. By then, there were no pottery-makers or pewterers — but still 13 watch and clock makers, and among other industries, there were listed 11 brassfounders, 72 cloggers, 39 coal proprietors, 17 cotton spinners, 12 iron and tinplate workers, 3 manufacturers of cotton goods, 14 mining engineers and surveyors, and 4 safety lamp makers.

It is also relevant to note that there were 15 breweries, 286 inns and public houses, and 284 retailers of beer. The Rev. Wickham, teetotaller and strong campaigner for abstinence from alcohol, was very much a Daniel in the lion's den.

At this time, the population of Wigan was around 50,000 of whom 11,000 or more were colliers. Many of the working population were children aged 10 to 12 years; and many women were working, either as 'pit brow lasses' doing heavy work at the surface of collieries, or in the cotton mills.

As for St. Andrew's Parish, this had been separated as a Peel District in 1870, with the union of an outlying district of All Saints Wigan and the hamlet of Marsh Green in the parish of Pemberton. The total population was about 1,000 — mostly colliers, mill-workers, foundry-workers, etc., and their families.

The two portions of the parish were separated by the railway, the canal, and the River Douglas, which in winter regularly overflowed its banks. Furthermore, as an article in the 'Illustrated Church News' for February 7th, 1896, put it (writing about the development of the church in Wigan), "The Wigan and Marsh Green people loved one another nearly as much as the Jews loved the Samaritans".

At the time, educational facilities in the parish were confined to a tumbledown school building at Marsh Green, coping with 60 children, and another small school building on the Wigan side, taking 40 children.

By 1872 the first minister of St. Andrew's, the Rev. A. A. K. Legge, had built a school-cum-church at Martland Bridge. By the time he resigned, in 1878, he had also built a small infant school and had raised about £1,000 towards the erection of a parish church. A site had been found and an architect engaged.

In 1881 St. Andrew's Ward had a population of 1,897, packed into 304 houses, so that was roughly the position found by Mr. Wickham, on his arrival Wigan in November 1878. As many of the houses were poor-quality terrace-type, built to site workers near their work, there was considerable overcrowding.

The report on the 'Pottery' (an area of low-class housing), made in 1879 by the Medical Officer of Health on the order of the Sanitary and Sewage Committees, gives a stark picture of the dreadful conditions in that part of the parish at the time.

"The Pottery covers an area of about two or three acres of low-lying land in the South district of the Borough, bounded by the canal on one side; and the [river] Douglas on the other, and contains in all 53 dwellings and over 300 inhabitants...

"...The dwellings consist mostly of four rooms...the kitchens in the Pottery (proper) are almost invariably below the surface of the ground. Many of the cottages are dilapidated, some with bulging-out walls, most with defective roofage and an almost total absence of spouting...there is no system of sewers...and, after a slow meandering, the sludge empties itself into the canal; or, after a more stagnant course, into the more adjacent river Douglas."

Commenting on the lack of water supplies, the 'closets' and paving, the report deals with slop disposal.

"Not more than two or three dwellings in the district have slop-stones, and these only serve to convey the slops just outside the house wall, where they form a half-stagnant gutter. The rest of the inhabitants throw their slops on the ground, in front of the house, where they lie either until the porous soil absorbs them, or until they are evaporated."

The general conclusion was "...the dwellings are of the poorest character...and tenanted by canal boatmen's families or factory operatives. They are, as may be inferred...damp...and unhealthy."

This, then, was Mr. Wickham's inheritance.

Chapter 4

*THE BUILDING VICAR*

## 1. St. Andrew's Church

Until 1882, all church services were held at the Martland Bridge School-cum-Church. The music was provided by the schoolmaster, Mr. Haworth, with his fiddle and the Vicar, Mr. Wickham, with his double-bass.

Upon his arrival in Wigan, Mr. Wickham wasted no time in getting down to the urgent need to provide a church. He was not at all happy with the plans drawn up; they were for a lofty church, expensive to build. Nor did he care for the proposed site, near to engine sheds and rolling mills and on ground he considered unsafe, due to mining operations. His third objection, as a teetotaller, was the nearness of several public houses.

So it was agreed he pay off the architect who, after a lengthy wrangle, accepted £100 as settlement. (Mr. Wickham had already been through the same experience at Talke-o-the-Hill.) Attracted to a church (St. Anne's) which a Mr Hunt of London had built at Derby, the Vicar engaged him and asked him to build a similar one. There were some modifications, the main one being the inclusion of an East window similar to the West window at Dunblane Cathedral.

It should be mentioned that Mr. Wickham maintained a lively interest in design and architecture. His reading included 'Building News', and there still exists a substantial volume, bound in 1881, and titled 'Architectural Studies'. Full of drawings and plans, there is everything from Anglo-Japanese furniture to Haddon Hall, Dunblane Cathedral, designs for stained glass at Fairford and Bledington, and a Bishop's chair, a font and a shrine at Hereford Cathedral.

The appeal for funds to build a church was launched on the basis of 'A Parish Church for a poor parish without one'. Despite the innumerable begging letters, and invitations to almost every person of consequence to act on the Building Committee, seven months of appeal work raised only £72. Acting on the principle that evidence of intent would be the best stimulus, building started on May 21st, 1879. The foundation stone was laid on June 3rd and work progressed until September 1880 when stopped by lack of funds. By then, the shell of the nave and chancel had been roofed in, but £600 was needed for work to re-start — and a further 20,000 letters were sent country-wide, couched in desperate terms; the response was not good. A big coal strike in the spring of 1881 was a further handicap to fund-raising; by the time building did re-start, in 1882, gales had done some damage to the roof and to two windows. As an economy measure it was decided to put open benches of pitch pine in the church instead of chairs.

Mr. Wickham was determined from the first to have a chancel screen to separate the two symbolisms of nave and sanctuary. The then Bishop of Liverpool expressed the view that anything would do — even a rope. Mr. Wickham declared that a rope would not even keep out a dog.

On August 1st, 1882, Dr. Ryle, Lord Bishop of Liverpool, con-secrated the church. During the ceremony a dog entered by an open door, trotted up the aisle into the Sanctuary and, after a brief inspec-tion of the officiating clergy (which included the Rev. Martyn Wickham, brother of the Vicar), trotted off again!

The church interior had a bare look about it during the early years. The first chancel screen was of wood painted in light colours. By the pulpit, and given by the architect, was the hour-glass. On its placement, the Vicar said of it, "It is a useful gift; and one which will serve a mystical as well as a practical purpose, reminding us in a forcible way of how the precious minutes of our lifetime — like the grains of sand . . . are running out".

Gradually, over many years, by congregational subscription, by outside donation and as private memorials, the ornaments and the furniture of the church were acquired. All the church furniture is of oak, beautifully carved. A very happy association had been established between the Vicar and a Mr. Advent Hunstone of Tideswell, in Derbyshire, an ecclesiastical carver; Mr. Wickham commissioned the pieces and provided rough sketches on which Mr. Hunstone worked with great skill and imagination. On one occasion, the Vicar had been concerned that not enough had been charged for a piece of work, bearing in mind the length of time taken to carve it; he wrote Mr. Hunstone accordingly. The reply came, "I am being more than well paid, for this work is teaching me the dignity of my craft".

The church is styled after the Early English period, "when men built as high as they dared". Especial features are the clerestory windows, pointed arches, a roof supported by king-post trusses, and a bell-tower. The bell was made in the Haigh foundry in 1835 and was given by the Wigan Coal and Iron Foundry.

Of particular mention are the pew-end carvings for the choir stalls: beauty in miniature. One is of Saint Cecilia playing an organ, with a little figure in cassock and surplice pumping away at the side. It was Advent Hunstone's 'conceit' (as Mr. Wickham called it) which caused him to carve, on the back of the organ, a cap and coat hanging from pegs.

The font is an exact copy of the almost unique Early English decagon font of Tingrith church, in Bedfordshire. It was provided by two Tingrith sisters, Nelly and Edith Hall, and from collections made by the Sunday School children. There are beautiful misericords in the Vicar's stall and the opposite stall, the first being a copy of one in Wells Cathedral.

The chancel screen, installed in 1902 to replace the original one, is a memorial to Mr. William Bryham, a great worker for and bene-factor to St. Andrew's. Together with the carved communion rail (based on a marble balustrade on a Venetian palace, seen and sketched by the Vicar whilst on holiday there), a personal memorial from his widow, they add splendidly to the furnishings.

All had good cause to remember Mr. Bryham for it was he who, at a time of great financial crisis, loaned the church £500 without any security. At the time, Mr. Wickham wrote, "The relief to myself was great indeed; we had quite come to the end of our money. The contractor had to be paid, and there was nothing to pay with. But for Mr. Bryham's kind offer, we must have come to grief." For many years, Mr. Bryham was Manager of the Douglas Bank Colliery and it was in all probability through his influence that the Colliery did so much for the church and for the schools, by way of money, resources and labour.

In the course of his address at the 1881 parochial tea party the Vicar dealt with criticisms that he had 'rushed into debt', stating that it was rare for a church to be built with money already raised. He concluded "We live in hope — filled also with a 'lively' sense of favours yet to come". They came. The lectern, bought in 1909 by congregational subscription, is a splendid piece of work. The eagle is of old oak, the base of an Austrian wainscot, and the shaft of brown oak from the park at Hardwick Hall. The eagle was given by Advent Hunstone, who only charged a nominal sum for the remainder of the work. Reporting its arrival in the August 1909 issue of the Parish Magazine Mr. Wickham wrote with great authority on the history and antiquity of eagle lecterns. The beautifully-carved Litany desk is a memorial to Mrs. Ann Brown, first caretaker of the church. The choir stalls, presented by the congregation in memory of a much-loved parishioner who died after a tragic accident, were added in 1894. The congregation also presented the panelling on the north wall of the Sanctuary, in memory of Mrs. Turner-Greene, another generous benefactor in Mr. Wickham's time.

Some idea of the tenuous financial situation may be gleaned from the St. Andrew's Annual Accounts. In 1881 income, other than specific donations for special causes, was £55 7s 7d. This was largely disposed of as £12 16s 2d to the School Fund, £15 6s 7d to the Building Fund, and £7 6s 2d to the Society for the Propagation of the Gospel.

Ten years later the comparable income had only grown to £105 3s 3d, of which just £11 1s 4d went to reserve.

In the event, the church cost only £4,500 and was finally cleared of debt by February 1886. This included the building, initial furnishings, and the heating system.


## 2. The Schools

Mr. Wickham, who had taken over very little by way of educational facilities, wrote at great length on the matter of 'Free education' in the June 1893 issue of the parish magazine. It is worth reproducing as it sets the scene clearly, concisely, and fairly.

"The present time seems fitting to say a few words to the parents of children attending St. Andrew's School, with respect to 'FREE EDUCATION'. By the Elementary Education Act of 1891, you are entitled to claim free education for your children. But, by the same Act, the Managers are entitled to charge school fees to the extent of 5s per annum. This is because, before the passing of the Act, our average fee was 15s. The Act allowed us only 10s a head of this, but left us the right to charge the remaining 5s.

"We therefore charge you the reduced fee of 1d per week for the first 3 standards, and 2d a week for the others, all the infants being free. In no case will all the children of one family be charged more than 3d a week. If your are unwilling to pay this fee, you can write to the Minister of Education in London and claim free education, and he has promised to see that you get it.

"How can he give it to you?

"He cannot give it to you in our school, against our will. He admits this...he then goes on to point the way...these are his words... 'If the demand for free places is not fully met by voluntary action, the School Board will be ordered to provide a free school or schools, within a reasonable distance of every child who has failed to obtain free education'."

'St. Andrew's Church, Wigan: East Aspect'. 1882. (L.S.)

'Interior view of St. Andrew's Church' (1882), showing the original painted screen; all was plain and utilitarian. (Very faded and yellowed. A.P.)

'Detail of the Bryham Memorial Screen', with 'Lincoln Imp' at left (grotesque, representing evil man, now converted, signifying the final triumph of Christ over all evil), 1902. (A.P.)

*'The St. Andrew's Schools, Wigan.' Copy of artist's drawing, reproduced in the 'Church Illustrated News', 1896.*

*'Angel playing a stringed instrument': pew-end carving, in choir stalls, 1892. (A.P.)*

*'The Litany Desk.' Memorial to Mrs. Ann Brown, the first St. Andrew's Church cleaner, 1898. (A.P.)*

'Advent Hunstone carving, watched by a nephew.' From an original photograph by a Tideswell photographer, 1903.

'The Eagle Lectern.' Paid for by congregational subscription, 1909 (see text). (Photo by K. Ward.)

'Misericord' in choir stalls, featuring heads of a King and a Bishop (Church and State united in God's work and worship). Misericords arose out of consideration for age and infirmity, allowing people to rest, whilst appearing to stand. (Photo by K. Ward.)

'St. Cecilia at organ with little blower': pew-end carving.

'Reverse of St. Cecilia pew-end carving, showing the coat and cap carved in by Advent Hunstone — a touch of his humour.'

Detail of choir-stall pew, with 'poppy-head.'
'David playing his harp': pew-end carving.
(Photographs on this page by K. Ward.)

The Vicar continued, "Mr. Acland can thus fulfil his promise . . . only by ordering the erection of a BOARD SCHOOL. Do you wish to have a Board School here? If you had one.

1. YOUR CHILDREN WOULD HAVE NO BETTER SECULAR EDUCATION THAN THEY HAVE NOW . . . according to the Blue Book of 1892, we are some way ahead of the Shevington Board Schools (two, built in a neighbouring parish, at considerable expense to the rate-payers).

2. THERE WOULD BE NO SECURITY THAT THERE WOULD BE ANY RELIGIOUS INSTRUCTION, which is the most important part of education. At Shevington there is none whatever. This is the case in many Board Schools. In others, there is Bible reading only without any explanation . . .

3. There would SOON BE A HEAVY RATE . . . AND YOUR RENTS WOULD BE RAISED — certainly not less than 3d a week, and probably more. And, remember, you would always have to pay this, whether you had children at school or not.

"What then would you gain, if Mr. Acland gives you 'Free Education' in a Board School? Will it not pay you better to continue to support our schools, and to send the small school fee and to let what is called 'Free Education' alone? We will promise that any parent who is really in need shall get his children educated for nothing, until he can afford to pay the fee."

The Vicar followed this up, in the next issue of the parish magazine, by quoting at length from Lord Halifax on the importance of religious education.

In February 1894, Mr. Wickham received a letter from the Education Department, following the visit of H.M. Inspector to the schools. This heavily criticised the structural state of them and intimated that no further grant would be made to the Infant School unless some assurance of new building was received.

The Vicar acted without delay. He set out the position in the March issue of the magazine: briefly, if no day schools then no Sunday schools and, later, a Board School and an increased rate burden for all through their rents. He asked for £2,000 for building and formed a Building Committee; £425 was quickly given or promised. A builder was engaged and the laying of the foundation stone fixed for June 6th.

Such was the confidence of the Building Committee that, following the laying of the foundation stone, a further decision was taken to build both the Infant School (for 177 children) and a Mixed School (for 276 children). In the space of two months, £1,917 10s 6d had been given or promised, leaving about £800 needed. Work went ahead splendidly and the schools were opened on November

28th. Later, both schools were extended and new facilities added, the Mixed School eventually taking 586 children.

The indebtedness was to continue for some years and cause the Vicar to launch himself into a fund-raising venture that, nearly 100 years later, has provided valuable photographic archive material for the nation. More of that, later.

## 3. The Vicarage

At the 1884 St. Andrew's annual tea party, the Vicar spoke of the need to build a vicarage (at this time he was a yearly tenant of a house outside the parish). He mentioned that, although he only wanted a small house, the Ecclesiastical Commissioners in their wisdom had reminded him that some day his situation might change. He must, therefore, build a house large enough for a clergyman's family; they would provide half the money.

The Vicar went on, "They mean to be very kind to us, I have no doubt, but... I fear they have killed... my chances... with kindness — like the elephant who unfortunately put his foot upon a hen partridge, and in his sorrow endeavoured to console her orphaned dear ones by sitting upon them as he had seen their mother do. He was extremely kind, but he killed them all."

At the time £1,400 was needed of which only £403 was in hand. Building eventually began in 1896 and in January 1897 the Vicar (now married) moved in with his family. By then the building had cost £2,732.

The April 1897 issue of the parish magazine devoted a lot of space to the Vicar's essay on the bill for the vicarage. Read in isolation from other material it could just have easily been lifted straight out of 'Punch'. It read as follows:

"We have at length received the bill for the vicarage. At the moment of writing, it has not been checked by the architect and until this has been done we cannot say exactly what the debt will be. But it will certainly be much larger than we expected, and may reach the sum of £160 or more. This is so serious a matter, in this poor parish, that we must think before we say anything more about it.

"Building is delightful work. But builders accounts are disagreeable. They are very wonderful, and the builders clerks do their best to make them interesting. The bill for St. Andrew's vicarage covers 21 closely-written foolscap pages — all of them crowded with information.

"First comes the amount of the contract in a lump sum — and then many a long page of extras, with some deductions. It is a 'give and take' business, but with a great deal more taking than giving. The account ebbs and flows like the tide, but, alas, the incoming tide.

"There is not a screw, not a bit of wood but is not carefully put down. Every unusual brick is there, too, and every load of ashes (what memories these builders have!). And the *time.* One begins to estimate aright the value of time, when one has to do with a builders account. Those fleeting hours — they all mean money. And the half-hours count up, too — they are never forgotten.

"Here is a wonderful item — one work at the vicarage took 798½ hours to do, at 10d an hour. That odd half-hour! It gives one confidence to find such care taken of it, but it also fills one with despair.

"There is but little chance of finding flaws (to one's advantage) in such a minutely-kept account. What becomes of the odd *quarters* of hours? The bill does not mention them. Possibly no building work can be done in so short a time or (the thought comes to one) the kind builder may scorn to charge for so small a portion of time, and worth only 2½d. And yet he does not despise half-pence by any means. The builder is even so accurate as to insert such an item as this: £2 10s 11½d. What could be more careful?

"Moreover, one has in the bill a most interesting record of the names of the people employed on the work. Sometimes, it is true, they are lumped ignominiously together, thus: Joiners 798½ hours at 10d; and, then again, Apprentices 9 hours at 5d; and, once more, Labourers 14½ hours at 7d. But sometimes the bill is much more particular, and tells us not merely the surname but also the Christian name of the workman.

"One has the satisfaction of knowing, and indeed of having a permanent record of the fact that Peter Winkles worked for 5½ hours at a wall in the drying ground, and got 10d an hour for his work; whilst Benjamin Rowbey worked the same time, but only got 6d an hour, though his mate, Patrick Begorrah got 7d. All this is very interesting, though one does not see why Peter Winkles, Benjamin Rowbey and Patrick Begorrah should have their names inserted, and not the rest.

"Perhaps they are especially good workmen. But then, on the other hand, all the workmen are specially good — none others are employed. The builder gives all these minute particulars — of screws, and names, and half-hours, and half-pence — to give one confidence.

"How can a bill be in the least excessive which is so carefully compiled? At any rate, we shall have to think about this particular bill, and of how it is to be paid. ONE HUNDRED AND SIXTY POUNDS or more to be found! We shall have to think".

The Vicar was obviously taken to task for his saucy treatment of the bill; and replied, in the next magazine issue.

"One or two of the Vicar's friends have rather objected to his little article on the vicarage bill, which seemed to them flippant. They thought he ought to take things more seriously.

"He begs to assure them he is perfectly serious. The article was an attempt to prevent him from becoming too serious. It was written partly to enable him to keep his spirits up, and not to lose heart.

"The debt on the vicarage is truly a most serious thing, and enough to make even a hopeful person depressed, especially when we remember that the school building debt is more than as much as the vicarage debt. To pay off both debts we need nearly four hundred pounds..."

(The vicarage debt was finally extinguished in March 1899, with a cheque for £50 from Mrs. Turner-Greene.)

Later, the Vicar described his new home as a "substantial, convenient, windswept and sunny building". As usual, he had devoted a great deal of thought to what was needed and it turned out to be a fine family house.

It was more than that for, with the conversion of a housemaid's closet equipped with a sink and running water, the Vicar provided himself with a practical photographic dark-room.

By this time he had become an expert photographer and the owner of one of the newer-type bellows cameras. He had already taken many photographs, church architecture, general scenes, his parishioners street hawkers, miners, mill and foundry workers; photographs of value as a record of social history of the time. These will be dealt with more fully elsewhere in this book.

## 4. Other Developments

In 1908 the Church House was acquired for use as a Boy's Club, being conveyed to the Liverpool Diocesan Finance Committee; it had been built in 1899 as a Liberal Club. As was aptly put in 'This Is Your Church', a comprehensive review of the establishment of St. Andrew's Parish and the work of its Vicars to 1962, "With the acquisition of the Church House...the facilities of the Church for providing spiritual, educational and social leadership in the district were almost complete, conveniently and compactly placed on one area of land". A little later a gymnasium was added and a Men's Club was also inaugurated. The final development during the ministry of Mr. Wickham was the securing of a site for a new church at Beech Hill, to cater for the population growth in that area of Wigan.

Along with the building developments went the growth of church community activity: Band of Hope, Communicants Guild, Mother's Meeting, Men's Mutual Improvement Society, Evening Classes for Younger Women (pit brow lasses, mill girls, etc.), Classes for Girls, the Sunday Schools, and the Men's Bible Class.

There were waxings and wanings, dying-outs and resurrections. Strenuous efforts by both Mr. and Mrs. Wickham, along with devoted helpers, somehow kept things going.

When St. Andrew's Church was being built, contrary to custom the laying of the foundation-stone ceremony was carried out by *four* people, representing the Clergy, the Land-owners, the Employers of Labour, and the Wage-earners. It was Mr. Wickham's success in 'marrying' the resources, talents, energies, and devotions of these four distinct classes that in turn laid the foundations for 30 years of courageous undertakings, all eventually crowned with success.

After Mr. Wickham's death in 1929 the July issue of the parish magazine carried a lengthy appreciation by his old friend of 34 years' association, the School Headmaster, Mr. Haworth. In the course of it he wrote, "St. Andrew's owes everything of its parochial machinery to Mr. Wickham's foresight and determination. He was called the 'building vicar' and the clink of a brick-layer's trowel on a brick was sweet music to him."

Chapter 5

## PHOTOGRAPHY AND MR. WICKHAM

In the early 1850s, a small boy in a velvet suit, with lace-collared tunic, sat in a chair posing for a daguerreotype photograph. This is thought to be the earliest photograph of William Arthur Wickham.

In locating his place in photography it is worth recording, briefly, the early discoveries of images created by sunlight; and the rapid developments from the great landmark year of 1839.

As far back as the 17th century it was known that silver chemicals reacted with the sun. In 1727, a German professor of medicine pasted paper stencils on a flask of silver nitrate solution and exposed it to sunlight. When he removed the stencils, the shapes of them were left, surrounded by darkened solution. Was it the sun's *heat* or *light?* Repeating the experiment in an oven proved that *sunlight* caused the effect.

Thomas Wedgwood, youngest son of the great pottery-maker, experimented similarly, in the early 19th century. He sensitised materials with silver salts, then laid objects on them and put them in sunlight. Like Professor Schultze in Germany, he produced images — which soon faded, however.

The first true photographs were made by a French lithographer-inventor, one Joseph Niépce, around 1824. He used a kind of asphalt, coating sheets of pewter with it, then exposing the 'plates' to sunlight in a pin-hole camera. After leaving the camera on a verandah all day he removed the plate, washed off unaffected asphalt with lavender oil, and found he was left with a faint outline of buildings opposite the camera.

Another Frenchman, Daguerre, was also convinced that permanent pictures could be made from images 'captured' by a lens. He met Niépce, and they became partners in a venture to improve the lithographer's 'heliographic' process. Niépce died in 1833, leaving Daguerre to pursue the problem; and in January 1839, his new photographic process was presented to the French Academy of Sciences.

The images were called daguerreotypes. Sheets of copper, coated with silver, were exposed to iodine vapour to form silver iodide. These sensitised plates were then exposed in a camera to the subject matter. They were then 'developed' by exposure to mercury vapour. The mercury linked up with the silver, which had reacted to the light passing into the camera, to form a shiny alloy which made up the light areas of the image. The rest of the silver was dissolved off in a chemical 'fixer' solution, leaving the dark areas. The light and dark areas, jointly, made the image.

The drawbacks to this system were three-fold. First, the process was hazardous, mercury being a toxic chemical. Second, a considerable length of time was needed for an image to form. Sitters were required to keep position for about half an hour, head held in a concealed neck-rest; and special chairs were devised for child photography, with someone crouching down behind and holding the child through a hole in the back of the chair. Third, the image could not be reproduced.

The answer to the problem of reproducing permanent images came almost at the same time, from an English scientist, Henry Fox Talbot. He had gradually been drawn into the fascinating challenge of producing permanent images, starting with the modifying of a pin-hole camera (camera obscura) to produce an image on a screen, to improve outdoor sketching.

Since the 16th century this principle had been used for amusement — darkened rooms, with light passing through a small aperture in a wall to cast on to the opposite interior wall an inverted image of what was going on outside. From the 17th century onwards the idea had been used, in miniature, to enable artists and others to see and to trace or draw landscapes and other subject matter, in proportion and in perspective. Later 'pin-hole' cameras even included a lens to control the amount of light entering the box, and thus 'sharpen' the image.

In 1834, at Lacock Abbey, his ancestral home (where the Fox Talbot Museum is now housed), Fox Talbot began experimenting with sensitised papers, producing images of leaves, ferns, etc. These he called 'photogenic drawings'. Turning to the problem of making permanent images, he was led to the solution by a fellow scientist, Sir John Herschel, who suggested the use of a chemical called Sodium Thiosulphate to 'fix' them.

Fox Talbot next got a local carpenter to make him a number of small boxes into which he fitted lenses (mousetraps, his wife called them). These he dotted round the house, each with its piece of sensitised paper inside. He found that he could produce images, which it was then possible to 'fix' — and so the 'calotype' or paper negative was born.

He next experimented with the making of positive images from his 'negatives' — and discovered that, by waxing them with beeswax, the paper negatives became translucent, allowing light to pass through them on to another sheet of sensitised paper to produce a 'positive' image which, again, could be fixed. (Contact printing — I can still recall my father coming out of the garden shed, where he did his own amateurish processing, with wooden printing frames which he balanced on a window-sill, facing the sun — similarly to produce his paper positives from negatives.) The announcement of Daguerre's process forced Fox Talbot to come out with his own; his negative-positive process was presented to the Royal Institution of Great Britain just 21 days later.

However, calotypes had one drawback: the fibres in the paper were of varying thicknesses, so light passed through the 'negative' unevenly. In consequence, prints made from them lacked sharpness.

In 1847, a cousin of Niépce produced a process for coating glass plates with an emulsion of silver in egg-white. Later, the invention of collodion by a French chemist was an inadvertent catalyst for photography. It was used, initially, as a wound dressing, forming a flexible skin. Robert Bingham, a British chemist, saw the possibilities for photography. Collodion was poured onto a sheet of glass and manipulated to form a thin film. Then it was immersed in a silver solution to sensitise it and, whilst still wet (for it lost sensitivity, once dry) was put in the camera, exposed, and developed. Thus, 'wet-plate' photography was born.

This process cut down exposure times considerably and much great archival photography was accomplished by it, until the discovery of gelatin led to the development of the 'dry' plate — a glass plate coated with a silver-sensitised gelatin emulsion. This became commercially available, around 1880, and remained popular for many years. Eric Hosking, premier bird photographer, was using a Sanderson camera and dry plates, among other equipment, during his early years of work in this field.

So Mr. Wickham, if he recalled his childhood experience, would remember the day when, for possibly half an hour, he had to sit still and look straight into the camera lens of a Mr. Abrahams. And how, later, he saw his image in the silvery-greys and black of a daguerreotype.

Certainly, by 1869, he had some knowledge of the next important development in photography — the 'View' camera; his photographs of, for instance, Winchester Cathedral, Netley Abbey,

*'Collier waiting': Wigan, 1891. (O.G.P.). Note safety lamp hooked on jacket; and 'hump' below ('snap-can' hooked on to trouser belt).*

*'Anxious faces, interested faces.' Taken at the St. Andrew's Soup Kitchen, 1893. (O.G.P.)*

'Collier "keawring" ' (squatting), 1891. (O.G.P.)

*'Old lady in doorway', 1891. (O.G.P.)*

*'Cruachan Burn', pre-1884. (A.P.)*

*'Yacht at Oban', pre-1884. (A.P.)*

Old Southampton Walls, and the exterior and interior of Romsey Abbey testify to that.

The View camera was simply a double-wooden box on a heavy wooden tripod. The inner box, which carried the lens, slid backwards and forwards to bring the subject matter into focus. For wet-plate photography out of doors the sensitised plates were loaded into the camera in a portable 'dark-tent', and the camera was taken into the tent again for the unloading and processing of the plate. Once the picture was composed and the camera set up, the photographer simply took off the lens-cap, timed the exposure, and replaced the cap. This process was really only suited to the studio, presenting major problems out of doors.

By the time Mr. Wickham became engaged in serious photography he had the benefit of the bellows-type field camera which took dry plates of smaller dimensions, and was much more portable. Such a camera could be bought for about £6, and plates and other equipment and chemicals in proportion.

His camera was probably a Lancaster or Sanderson; his daughters well remember him focusing the camera under a black cloth. It was probably equipped with a rising front and swing-back operation to correct the verticals. This would explain why his photographs of abbeys, cathedrals, etc., show no perspective distortion. He was certainly one of the earliest photographers to record some of the social history of the time, his coal strike photographs and those taken around his parish and down the pit being not all that far behind the published London scenes of John Thomson (1877). Thomson's was the first serious attempt, in England, to supplement social commentary with photography: in his case, to draw attention to urban poverty in London. Splendid, telling pictures they were, beautifully composed.

Looking at Mr. Wickham's photographs, it is well to bear in mind all the problems of the 19th century photographer, despite the improvements in both technique and equipment, already made by his day.

Photographic emulsions were more 'grainy' than now, calling for relatively long exposures; whilst finished prints lacked the range of tonality from black to white which can nowadays be achieved. Long exposures posed no problems when the subject matter was inanimate, other than that caused by changes in natural lighting outdoors; but try to pose someone on a snowy slope whilst you get under the black cloth to compose the picture, focus it, take out the viewing screen and slip in a negative plate, then expose it, and everything is against a final sharp image. Try to photograph a group of people and someone is bound to move.

Also, there was not much in the way of processing chemicals and, dependent upon storage conditions, stated amounts of those available could be right or wrong. Some used were inclined to dry out, becoming stronger per set weight, and others to absorb water and become weaker. Such chemicals were used by Mr. Wickham — we still have some of his working formulae. So processing was less precise than nowadays, setting odds against perfection.

Camera lenses, although much improved with the introduction of the Petzval lens, which became the photographer's standard lens and revolutionised photography, were a long way behind the performance of modern lenses.

Take all these disadvantages, add the sheer physical exertion of carrying around a heavy camera and tripod, plus a box of glass plates — and the 19th century photography of Mr. Wickham and others becomes a feat of great skill, stamina, and patience. In addition, there was the matter of 'rapport' with the subject or subjects, to produce a picture that appeared to be unposed. Mr. Wickham seemed to have the happy knack of getting people to forget he and his camera were there, and he made the best of the situation to get simple, contrasty compositions: Bernard standing in the vicarage doorway is a typical example.

It is unfortunate that his great talent was not recognised before hundreds of photographs he took in Wigan and elsewhere were discarded, or deteriorated beyond saving. On the other hand, it is good to know that, almost 100 years on, some of his work is adding to our visual knowledge of life in his time. From the 500 or so photographs left, there still may be other contributions to be made.

Chapter 6


## *THE LANTERN SHOWS*

Lantern shows were first used for public entertainment in this country in the 1850s — usually at fairs. The apparatus could project pictures up to 20 feet square from the small, usually painted, glass slides.

The first evidence we have of lantern shows in the St. Andrew's parish comes in an announcement in the April 1886 issue of the magazine.

"ON MONDAY APRIL 12th at 7.30 p.m. in the MARTLAND BRIDGE SCHOOL, MR. BELL of LIVERPOOL will exhibit his famous OXYHYDROGEN LIMELIGHT TRI-UNIAL LANTERN, with the CYCLOIDOTROPE or INVISIBLE DRAWING MASTER and the KALEIDOSCOPE. Mr. Bell will also tell the Temperance Story called 'Given in Charge' or Little Joy's Mission, with illustrations from Life Models. There will also be Dissolving Views and Comic Scenes."

This attraction was to be a 'grand wind up' for the winter season of the Temperance Society and the Band of Hope.

The principle of illumination was the use of a flaming jet of oxygen and hydrogen gases directed on to a disc of lime, heating it to brilliant incandescence. Apart from the fire hazard, other practical problems (to judge from the Vicar's notes on lantern shows that were not successful) were (1) gas bottle — later, gas cylinder — running out, (2) inadequate intensity of light, (3) light disc too large and only part of the slides projected.

Subsequently lantern shows became a regular feature of entertainment in the parish, usually given in the school but, on occasion, in the church, for devotional purposes. During Lent, 1888, a series attracted an average attendance of 143!

The vicar, writing of the novelty of lantern shows, especially in churches, said, "There can be no more real objection on principle to a Lantern Service in church than to a stained glass window. The

Church has always instructed its children, when possible, by means of the eye..."

Later, Mr. Wickham was loaned slides of Switzerland and used them to talk about his holiday there. Next was the children's turn, with comic slides borrowed from Liverpool. Then the Vicar went to Wigan infirmary and gave a show in one of the wards, packed with patients and staff. This became an annual event for a time; Mr. Wickham commented, "More might be done than is done to amuse the patients...the nurses, too, lead a monotonous life and an occasional entertainment would brighten it up a little".

In November 1889 the Vicar gave a show of slides made for him after a holiday in Belgium, and 1890, of a holiday in Holland and Germany. On this latter occasion the oxygen bottle ran out! Everyone present was given a pass-out and came back the following night when the show went off without trouble. All these shows and others were for the purpose of fund-raising.

In 1890/91 Mr. Wickham decided to tackle a big lantern show project with the object of raising money to reduce the debt on the schools; the situation there was getting worse as expenses were exceeding income. He had been disappointed with attendances at 'educational' shows, which had included coloured slides of famous places and sights of the world, and a series on China. He would let the people of the parish see themselves on the screen. For many months he and Mr. Haworth went round the parish taking photographs: on the streets, into homes, mills, foundries, to the collieries, to the canal, into the church, and to parish events.

Then came the arduous task of converting the pictures into lantern slides but at last all was ready: over 160 photographs. The September 1891 issue of the parish magazine carried the details, including 'a remarkable series of views taken by flash-light in the pit'.

The Public Hall at Wigan had been taken for the show and following the announcement 'Carriages may be ordered for 10 o'clock', the vicar added, "The thing we want to avoid is cramming the room so full that no one will be able to laugh".

On the night all the seats were taken, many people had to stand, and many were turned away. Heartened, Mr. Wickham decided to repeat the show twice in Wigan and then took it to Southport, but it was not very successful.

Less than half the lantern slides remain and most of the original glass plate negatives have gone. Even so, it is possible to gauge the remarkable photographic accomplishment of Mr. Wickham from the residue , a selection from which is shown here. Some background information is provided for the appreciation of the canal boat scenes and the underground colliery pictures.

## Photography at the Leeds—Liverpool Canal

On October 23rd, 1816, the Leeds—Liverpool Canal was opened. It covered 127 miles, crossed the Pennines, made use of water from seven reservoirs, and included 91 locks and two tunnels. It was the culmination of a great feat of engineering that occupied nearly 50 years. In 1821, following earlier extensions, the opening of the Leigh branch canal, linking Leigh and Wigan, linked up the extensive Midlands waterway systems and made possible the carriage by waterway of coal, grain, cotton, and a variety of other 'goods'.

Wigan became an important terminus and the families of boatmen were to be found housed in cottages near the canal. In the 1871 Census it is recorded that, in addition, 93 people were living on 30 boats at Crooke pier on the outskirts of Wigan. The piers, incidentally, were a series of ramps linked to colliery tramway systems, positioned at the canal-side to enable the contents of wagons to be tipped directly into boats.

By the 1850s competition from the railways began to make itself felt. Later in the century a series of summer droughts followed by a very severe winter in 1895 closed the canal for long periods, driving traffic away. Despite many improvements, continuing troubles such as canal bursts hastened the decline of the canal. Nevertheless, at the time of Mr. Wickham's photography, it was a very busy waterway.

The photographs show two interesting features. In some, a representative of the London City Mission, dressed as Father Christmas and accompanied by a small retinue in fancy dress, is distributing gifts to children on the boats. This organisation has confirmed that it was the practice to do so, not necessarily confined to the London river area. A Mr. Charles Woodall was their missionary to barge-folk at the time, so perhaps this is he.

A very nautical-looking gentleman also appears on a number of the photographs: first, with what is obviously a group of civic dignitaries on a tour of inspection; and, again, handing out what are presumably certificates of clearance. He was probably the examiner at Wigan, reporting on the condition of boats and making recommendations to put right faults.

There were two types of boat, 'wide' and 'narrow'. The examining officer's report embraced the nature of the traffic carried, the number of cabins and their condition, ventilation, storage, sleeping accommodation, type of stove, special provision for foul cargo (remarkably, manure seems to have been popular traffic), and facilities for storing at least three gallons of drinking water. It was also necessary to state whether the boat was to be registered and used as a dwelling.

'Steering gear': taken near Wigan, 1891 (L.S.). The 'gathered' bonnet of the tiller-woman appears on numerous photos.

'The fish hawker': Wigan, 1891. (O.G.P.)

*'Good news or bad?': receiving the Boat Examiner's report, 1891. (L.S.)*

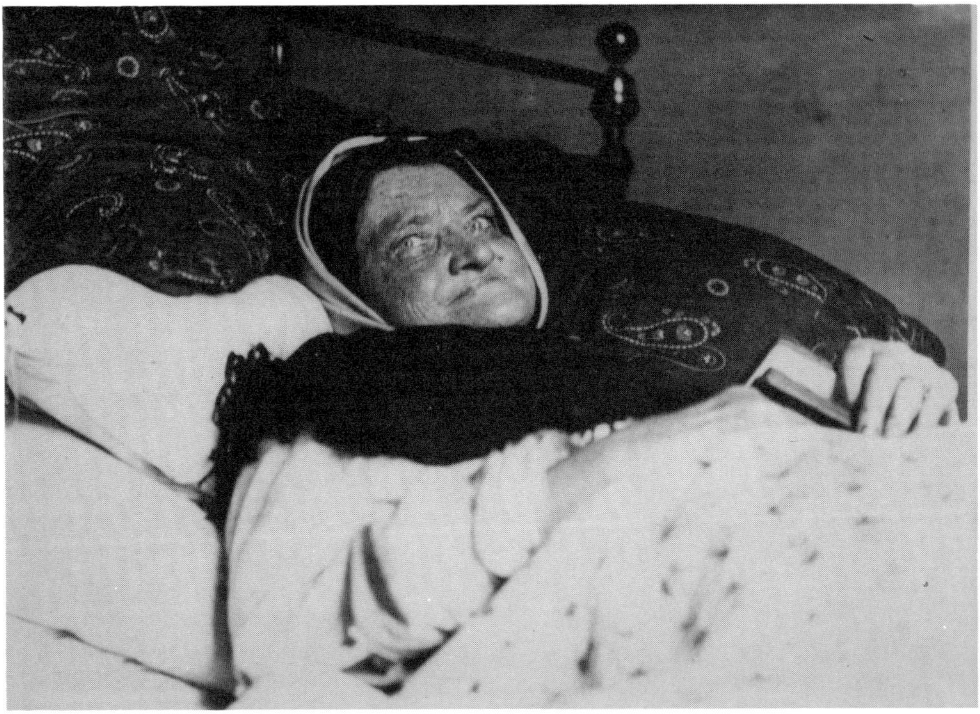

*'Elderly parishioner in bed': Wigan, 1891. (O.G.P.)*

*'Christmastide.' City of London Mission representative distributing gifts to boat children, 1891. (L.S.)*

*'The bread oven': Wigan, 1891. (L.S.)*

*'Wash-day in the alley': back-to-back cottages in the parish, 1891. (L.S.)*

*'St. Andrew's Mothers' Meeting'; dressed up for an outing, 1891. (O.G.P.)*

Mr. Wickham's collection has added substantially to presently available photography of life on the canal towards the end of the 19th century.

## Photography below ground, at the Douglas Bank Colliery

The first-known attempt to take photographs down a mine in this country took place in 1864. Then during 1881—82, Arthur Sopwith, a mining engineer, took a series of pictures down a pit in South Staffordshire.

The immediate questions that posed themselves to me, on seeing the lantern slides, were:

(a)  How did Mr. Wickham know how to tackle it?
(b)  How did he cope with the practical photographic problems?
(c)  How serious were the hazards of 'firedamp' (methane gas) explosion and/or coal-dust explosion?
(d)  What form did Mr. Wickham's 'flashlight' take?

Dealing with (a): the parish magazine for November 1891 probably provides the clue. Mentioning that he will be giving two repeat lantern shows, he adds, "Seventeen photographs taken in a pit in South Staffordshire have been added to the collection, and will probably prove of great interest".

Three of the existing lantern slides have positively been identified by the Science Museum (London) as underground scenes taken by Arthur Sopwith. Mr. Wickham went to Wigan from a colliery village in South Staffordshire and it seems reasonable to assume that he got to know Sopwith and, later, used the knowledge gained for his own photography: and borrowed some of Sopwith's photographs to convert to slides.

As to (b): apart from the problem of working with a bulky camera in the confined workings, the main difficulty would be lack of light for focusing. This is shown by the unsharpness of some of the photographs. The other problem was the *amount* of light needed to illuminate the scene. The tendancy would be to use the smallest calculated amount to reduce any hazard of secondary explosion. So we are left with some inadequately lit photographs and some of good exposure.

As regards (c): the writer's first thought was 'What a risk'. Dealing first with 'firedamp', investigation showed that methane concentration could be determined by rough-and-ready means.

'Firedamp', or methane gas, is a natural by-product of the formation of coal by the laying-down, some 300 million years ago, of layers of vegetable matter in the Carboniferous forests. Water-logged, subsequent compression from overlaying debris over a great period of time converted the vegetable matter first to peat and, later, to coal. Heat, generated during the process, produced the gas which was trapped in the coal. When released, as the coal-face was worked, and combined with the oxygen in the atmosphere *in sufficient amount,* it formed an explosive mixture.

Before the advent of the safety lamp, it was the practice for 'firemen', covered in water-soaked rags, to crawl to the coal-face on hands and knees with a candle on a pole — and present it upwards, where the pocket of gas had collected, so as to ignite it: a dangerous job. The Davey lamp, first candle-lit and later oil-lit, not only provided better illumination for the collier working the coal-face but enabled him to determine roughly the amount of 'firedamp' present — and, therefore, the degree of danger. Basically, the lamp was a light surrounded by a wire-gauze cage. Any gas entering the cage was burned off *inside it,* the heat so produced being conducted off quickly by the wire-gauze, so that the gas *outside* the lamp did not ignite. Provided that the shape of the flame did not exceed that of an equal-sided triangle, the level of 'firedamp' was acceptable.

Moreover, ventilation in pits at that time was still poor, keeping oxygen levels down. It was for this reason that the risk of a coal-dust explosion was minimal. Indeed, when better ventilating equipment was introduced into pits the number and extent of explosions increased and, for a time, miners agitated for a return to the older and safer conditions of work. It was also the practice to spray water, where practicable, to reduce the coal-dust explosion hazard. So it must be assumed that the authorities were satisfied that 'flashlight' photography was safe.

Finally, taking point (d)' how far had 'flashlight' photography progressed by 1891?

Artificial-light photography was first tried out in the 1850s. First, burning magnesium wire was used for illumination. This produced an extremely bright light, similar to daylight — but also a cloud of white smoke, unbearable to the photographers, which soon obscured the scene to be photographed.

Later, in the 1880s, came 'flash powder' usually a mixture of finely-ground magnesium with potassium chlorate. This was a hazardous material to handle and accidents to photographers and their assistants became an occupational risk.

The one advantage of 'flash powder' was that it tended to burn for a relatively long time — perhaps a second. This enabled the photographer to use a smaller aperture and extend the depth of focus, improving the prospects for a picture clear in detail.

We do not know just what Mr. Wickham used — nor whether, with his practical turn of mind and help from technicians at the colliery, a device was made to minimise the risks. Certainly he accomplished his task safely and successfully. His collection of photographs is the most comprehensive to be taken at a colliery in the 19th century in this country; and has added considerably to archive material of the time.

Apart from the many photographs taken underground, others embrace most aspects of a typical late-19th century colliery: 'pit brow lasses' at work, miners going down in the primitive cage, coal-tipping into barges, women grading coal on the shutes and shovelling coal at the railway sidings, the engine-man at work, a huge steam-shovel filling wagons — and so on. Also, some splendid character studies of colliers.

After 1891, there is little evidence of the continuance of lantern shows at St. Andrew's. Perhaps the Vicar was disappointed with the results — so much time, energy, and expense (for Mr. Wickham financed it all from his own pocket) for so little gained. Also, his time was being increasingly taken up in other directions. For demands on his varied talents were increasing: calls he regarded his duty to fulfil if humanly possible, as he was to tell his parishioners many years later, in his farewell letter to them.

Chapter 7

## *MARRIAGE AND FAMILY BACKGROUND*

On June 21st, 1892, the marriage of the Rev. W. A. Wickham and Miss Clara Peck was solemnised at St. Andrew's Church. The officiating clergy were the Rev. H. M. Wickham, Vicar of Alveley, in Shropshire, brother of Mr. Wickham; and the Rev. Gerard Finch, Hon. Fellow of Queen's College, Cambridge, uncle of the bride. It was a simple wedding and a plain service. Nevertheless, it was a great occasion for the parishioners, who thronged the church.

Two years previously, at the annual parochial tea party, the Vicar was reminiscing about his coming to Wigan. He had said, jokingly, referring to the many advantages "...there are very few weddings... which are unprofitable...only the very respectable are married at St. Andrew's; the riff-raff go by into Wigan" (great laughter). The parishioners certainly got a most respectable wedding; and we are greatly indebted to one of Clara's brothers, Dr. Herbert Peck, for details of her family.

Clara was the eighth of 15 children born of the union of John Henry Peck and Martha Finch. Clara's father was Wigan-born and, after a private education, was intended for a schoolmaster. But his father's death, when John was 15, necessitated the abandonment of the idea. Going into his father's business of sailmaker and tarpaulin manufacturer he did well, eventually buying out his brothers' interests and making it his own.

In 1856 he had entered Wigan Town Council as representative of All Saints Ward, with the two objects of securing the municipalisation of the gas and water undertakings and the redemption of the market dues then paid to the Rector of Wigan. This latter was the last of the rights granted to Rectors of Wigan in the 13th and 14th centuries. These objects John Peck eventually accomplished and he resigned from the Town Council. Later he was appointed to the Bench.

It is worth noting that he was a great 'fancier' and his business premises at Wallgate, Wigan, were said to resemble a menagerie. The breeding and showing of poultry was his principal hobby. He was the first to breed black Spanish fowl with white eye-lids and won many prizes with them and with Brahmas and Game Bantams. He was also a great hoaxer and once undertook to provide a game dinner for a party of friends during the close season. With the collaboration of the manager of the Victorial Hotel, he provided 'venison' in the form of a fore-quarter of fat mutton which, wrapped in a tarpaulin, had been buried for several days. Also 'partridges', bantams which had been strangled and hung for an appropriate time.

Clara's mother, Martha Peck, belonged to an old Wigan family and was the second child of John and Nancy Finch. She was a remarkably intelligent child for, on her third birthday, there was a family gathering to hear her read and to see a sampler worked by her. She, too, was privately educated. Herbert Peck records that "She appears to have been hard-worked, too hard-worked, all her life... but accepted good and trouble with equanimity, being supported throughout her life with a sincere and unquestioning faith". Despite the demands of the nursing and bringing-up of 15 children, Martha Peck found time to write poetry which appeared mostly in the local papers. She died in 1902 having outlived her husband by 14 years. The Pecks became parishioners of St. Andrew's when they moved to Gidlow Lodge. According to the surviving daughters of Mr. Wickham, when he first stated his serious intentions towards Clara he was given a kitten (? out of the Wallgate 'menagerie') and was told that if he could care for the kitten he would be considered for Clara. He succeeded — and 'Titchums', as he was called, lived to a ripe old age. We have photographs of him, stretched out comfortably in a basket chair.

It is thought that Mr. Wickham may have met Clara at a charity concert, where she was accompanying her sister Edith, who had trained at the London Academy of Music with the idea of taking up a singing career. (She changed her mind, married, and used her musical talent for charitable purposes only.) Mr. Wickham, living outside the parish of necessity, was at that time unable to offer Clara a home; later, thanks to the kindness of Mr. Bryham, he was able to remedy the matter.

Clara had been educated at private schools in Wigan, Southport, and at Pyrmont and Erfurt, in Germany (several of her sisters followed the same educational path). In 1884 she became an L.R.A.M., obtaining honours in the senior division. Of her brothers and sisters only one died in infancy, and most had remarkable careers. Singled out are those of Walter (for its uniqueness), Alfred, and Herbert, both of whom helped the Wickham family one way or another.

*Walter* was educated at private schools and at Wigan Grammar School. He received free Articles at the Haigh Foundry, Wigan, for the ability he had shown. He took a Queen's Prize for a design for a double-crank engine at the examination of Science Classes held by the Committee of the Privy Council on Education. In 1879 he went out to New Zealand and, after careers in agriculture, threshing and hauling, and marine engineering returned to England. In 1886 at Newcastle he took examinations and, within six weeks of each other, passed as chief and extra-chief engineer. Going back to New Zealand, he was, with the exception of one other person with similiar qualifications, the best-qualified engineer in Australasia. He eventually moved to Sydney, where he founded a College of Marine Engineering, practised as a consultant engineer, and was Secretary of the Sydney branch of the Australasian Institute of Marine Engineering from 1904 until his death in 1915.

*Alfred* had an almost identical education to Walter. Then he entered his father's business and worked his way up to become the managing director, after it was converted to a limited liability company. He conducted the business with great success for many years. Always identifying himself with social and charitable work, he was the principal supporter of all the local war charities during the 1914—18 war, and one of the prime movers in the erection of the town war memorial. In 1932 he gave over part of his business premises and, with the help of the Wigan Council for Social Service, established the Wigan Men's Occupational Centre and Club for the unemployed. This was formally opened by the then Prince of Wales whilst on a tour of Lancashire to see what was being done for the workless.

*Herbert* was edcuated at Wigan Grammar School and Hatton Hall, Dumfries, before going to Edinburgh University and Medical School, becoming M.D., M.B., C.M.(Ed.), L.R.C.S., L.R.C.P.(Ed) — and also D.P.H.(Cambridge) and barrister-at-law of Lincoln's Inn. He was one of the first doctors to use diphtheria anti-toxin; and it was largely through a paper compiled by him and read to the British Medical Association that the infectiousness of typhoid fever was recognised. His other interests were archaeology and numismatics: he was one of the best authorities on coins in the Midlands — and he wrote many papers on medical and archaeological subjects.

After his death, a memorial plate was put up in Hasland Church, Chesterfield, where he had been Medical Officer of Health for many years. At the memorial service, the Rural Dean said in his address, ''Dr. Peck was a great authority on sanitation and the prevention of disease...he was regarded as one of the greatest experts in the prevention and cure of smallpox and ...he helped to stamp out that terrible scourge in this country. He did great work in the establishment of Isolation Hospitals...and was foremost in the struggle to provide the public with pure water...and plenty of it.

"His ideas regarding slums and overcrowding were abreast of the times...we rank the late Dr. Peck as one of the greatest pioneers."

Dr. Monica Wickham recalls her uncle telling her of his early days as Medical Officer of Health. Vagrants usually spread variola major, the deadly form of smallpox and, after the discovery of a case, he would cycle around the countryside looking for the infected tramp. Apart from studying law in his spare moments as Medical Officer of Health, and his other activities, he still found time and energy to research the genealogy of the Pecks and the Finchs, eventually producing limited edition volumes of both for the families, who were traced back to the 16th century.

The writer is greatly indebted to his perseverance and capability for the wealth of detail on the members of Clara Peck's family, herself, and her forbears.

It is not known whether Clara had any money settled on her upon her marriage. Alfred Peck certainly gave financial help and the Pecks as a family were generous with gifts.

The children of the marriage of William Wickham and Clara Peck were Myrtle, who was born in 1893 and died in 1973; Bernard, born in 1894, and killed in France in 1917; and Cicely, Monica and Caroline, with whose consent and enthusiastic help this book was made possible.

*Bernard* was educated at Millmead, Shrewsbury, and at Christ's Hospital, which he entered by competition, taking first place on the list. He later became an Exhibitioner of the School, and of St. John's College, Cambridge, where he had completed his first year when the Great War broke out. He also held an Exhibition from the Grocer's Company. He was a member of the University O.T.C., and obtained his commission in September 1914, joining the South Staffordshire Regiment. He won the Military Cross for conspicuous gallantry in 1916, suffering wounds, was promoted to lieutenant in 1917 and, after illness and hospitalisation, returned to duty. He was killed by a sniper near Ypres, on April 14th 1917.

*Cicely* was educated at Casterton School, from 1905 to 1915, being a Waldegrave scholar for the last two years, which involved some teaching. She became head girl, captain at cricket and hockey, and a member of the tennis six. From 1915 to 1919, she was on the junior staff of St. Elphin's School, teaching music and acting as secretary to the headmistress. Subsequently, she became a trained secretary, taking a variety of posts to get a 'rounded' experience. Some time was spent at Ampton helping to look after her parents.

Whilst there, she became parish clerk and also organist at Ampton Church. During the First World War, she served for a time in the Red Cross, until illness prevented continuance.

*Monica* was educated at St. Elphin's School, from 1908 to 1919, before going to the Royal Free Hospital for Women to study medicine. In her final year she did a brief locum for her Uncle Herbert at his smallpox hospital in Chesterfield.

Qualifying M.B., B.S.(Lond.) in 1925, she first did locum work, then went as assistant in a Winsford practice. In 1928 she bought a practice in Sholing, Southampton. In those days, her 3s 6d fee covered a visit, full examination, and the cost of the medicine!

In 1929 she was appointed a Poor Law doctor and Public Vaccinator, which provided a welcome small additional income. She retired from general practice in 1954.

*Caroline* also went to St. Elphin's School, and from there to St. Thomas' Hospital, London, becoming an S.R.N. and also gaining the Certificate of the Central Midwives' Board. She then did a further training under the Queen's Institute of District Nursing, and became a Queen's Nurse, which was to be her life's work. From 1932 to 1933, she took an international course at Bedford College, London, which enabled her to gain her Health Visitor's Certificate. She was Superintendent of the Metropolitan Training Home for Queen's Nurses, from 1939 to 1944 and Superintendent of the Oxford Training Home from 1945 to 1955.

Following Monica's retirement from general practice, she and her sisters Cicely and Caroline established themselves in rural Hampshire; and now lead an independent yet collective life in a custom-built house, each with their own 'quarters' and garden, overlooking the Downs, at the top of a pretty old-world village.

# Chapter 8

## *HONEYMOON IN SWITZERLAND: 1892*

Mr. Wickham and his bride travelled to Folkestone — then on to Switzerland; their destination, was Bel Alp. He had been there before, in 1888, and this part of the Bernese Oberland, with the great Aletsch glacier, obviously held particular attraction for him.

This was to be no ordinary honeymoon. He took with him his cumbersome bellows-type camera and tripod and a good supply of glass photographic plates — no doubt with an eye to the possibility of reducing the cash deficit on one or other of the St. Andrew's building projects.

During their stay he took 107 photographs, recording subject matter and exposure in a little note-book. It is interesting to note that exposures varied from 'instantaneous', outdoors, to 30 minutes for the interior of a chapel.

We do not know how he determined exposure time; possibly with a Watkins 'Bee' lightmeter. This had two dials and a circle of sensitised paper, with a darkened fixed piece as a control. The time it took the sensitised paper to darken, when exposed to the same intensity of light as the subject matter, was translated into an exposure time by referring to the dials.

Mr. Wickham went about this photography with his usual thoroughness. He went on to the village streets to 'capture' local characters and scenes; up the mountains and on to the snows; even setting-up his equipment on the Aletsch glacier, with its hummocky, slippery surface.

The results speak for themselves. A few show subject movement (many of the exposures were of several seconds); some plates have suffered emulsion deterioration but, despite the ensuing 88 years, about 50 are still of good reproducible quality.

In the August, 1892 issue of the parish magazine the Vicar regaled his parishioners with a descriptive account of his holiday. He wrote, of the Aletsch Glacier... "It takes some little time to realise the facts when you stand and look down upon the Aletsch glacier for the first time. It looks very much like a snow-covered highway, with two trampled paths up the centre of it, and you think you are almost close to it, whereas it lies 2,000 feet below you.

"When, after a rapid walk of an hour, you reach it, you find what a giant you have to deal with — that its apparently smooth surface is broken by crevasses which go down into depths which a line 1,500 feet long might be unable to fathom — that the 'cinder paths' (as an American lady called them) are medial moraines, thickly strewn with boulders of great sizes. Altogether, you feel the glacier must be treated with respect.

"But when you get used to him and his icy ways — when you can feel your feet upon his surface, and look down into his crevasses, and leap across them or cross the bridges and knife-edges without giddiness — then you will find a great delight in glacier walking.

"You will need a good ice axe in your hand, a pair of blue goggles over your eyes, an ample white handkerchief around your hat, a stout pair of well-nailed boots on your feet — and plenty of cold cream on your face. . . .

"But when you have toiled . . . up again to the hotel, you will probably find that, in spite of all your precautions, the old glacier has given you some kisses which have left a sting behind them. When you look in the glass, you will be startled at the colour of your face, which will be nearer mahogany than flesh colour; and, for the next few days, you may expect an uneasy time of it, as your skin blisters and smarts and peels."

. . . and, of the ascent of the Beichgrat (10,300 feet), "Another day, we went up the Ober Aletsch glacier to the Beichgrat, and were for some hours completely in the snow world. We were securely roped together by way of precaution, for the glacier was deeply crevassed beneath the snow.

"We had a long and rather weary tramp, for the snow was soft,

but we were amply repaid by the views on every side of us; and, on the way down, we enjoyed some long glissades which shortened the journey. We were fortunate in securing as our guide Anton Walden, the leading guide in these parts and a most excellent fellow."

Mrs. Wickham had a notebook similar to her husband's, in which she recorded little anecdotes and happenings on the holiday. She wrote about Anton Walden . . . "One day, we went to Tony's chalet . . . and made the acquaintance of his wife. They have had two children, but both are dead. He owns the chalet he lives in — also 1½ others.

"We heard a story of Tony, a few days ago, and I asked him the truth of it. It is to the effect that he was once on the Aletschorn with a gentleman and a porter, when they were enveloped in mist and had

*'Chapel and Füsshorner.' (O.G.P.)*

*'Sunlight and Shade'; village scene. (O.G.P.)*

*'The ice table: the Aletsch Glacier.' (O.G.P.)*

55

'Helping hand,' Tony, the guide, assists Mrs. Wickham. (O.G.P.)

'Roped together': Mr. and Mrs. Wickham, with guide in between. Ascent of the Beichgrat (10,300 feet). (O.G.P.)

'Cautiously does it': Mrs. Wickham, feeling for a foot-hold. Tony, the guide, has moved his head. (O.G.P.)

e

'Guide at Ravine.' (O.G.P.)

'On the Aletsch Glacier': a badly deteriorated plate, but worthy of inclusion for the photographic challenge of setting up camera, on a tripod, on such hazardous terrain. (O.G.P.)

'Baggage transport at the hotel.' (O.G.P.)

to remain there for about 15 hours. They had plenty of provisions but could make no use of them, for they were frozen. They had no fire, and only had the lightning, which played around them, and especially their axes, to keep them warm."

Whilst at the Bel Alp Hotel, the Wickhams became friendly with a Roman Catholic priest who was responsible for the local community. They went to call on him. Mrs. Wickham again ... "Today we went to Bel Alp, a little hamlet about ¾ hour walk from the hotel, that we might call on the Roman Catholic priest there.

"He came up the mountain on Monday, to remain among the people here until the middle of September. He came towards us, welcoming us cordially ... and invited us into his chalet. He brought us milk, which we drank out of the bowl cups which are so common here.

"His chalet is very simply furnished, if furnished it can be called, for there was little besides a plain wooden table, a couple of wooden benches and a bed. There was a roughly-hewn stone 'ofen' (oven), making one wonder almost if it were an altar, for on it were the letters 'I.H.S.' and, below them 'C.S.', and a date, 1631.

"There were a few very poor pictures on the wall and, in one corner, a crucifix. On the table was a black, glazed jug with lovely wild flowers in it.

"He brought us a good length of the way back to the hotel, giving us some information concerning himself and his people. He was born at Naters, down below here, and has been Curé for six years.

"The children are bound to go to school in the winter months — but not in the summer; and undergo a stiff Government examination. The whole community is charged with their education. A teacher is paid 300 francs a year, and can live on it.

"He asked for a subscription to be started at the hotel, as has been the case in former years, for a fund for food for the poor children in the winter."

Mr. Wickham concluded the account of his holiday ... "The Vicar exposed about 100 plates but, until they are developed, the less said about them the better".

Any uncertainty he had as to the results must have been dispelled once he set to work on them in his dark-room.

# Chapter 9

*COAL-MINING AND THE COAL STRIKES*

Records of coal-mining in the Wigan area go back to the 14th century; and, by the beginning of the 17th century, there were numerous pits — shallow at first, but later going down to 100 feet or more. The practice was to work outwards from the shaft until the tunnel collapsed — then to start a new tunnel. The coal was filled into corves (shallow baskets); horse-power was used to haul up the baskets.

As pits got deeper, the hazards increased and conditions of working got worse. Pit-workers, men, women, and children suffered appallingly. There was no artificial ventilation; 'firedamp' (methane gas) and black damp or 'choke' (a mixture of carbon dioxide and nitrogen which would not support life) were common hazards. In turn, dogs, birds and mice were used to check for the presence of 'choke'. Hours of work were disgracefully long, and workers, especially the young, were often beaten to get more out of them; the work was filthy and perilous, undermining health and hazarding life and limb, and the pay (if such it can be called) scandalous.

The following, from an investigation carried out in 1841 by a Mr. J. L. Kennedy, are typical examples of work in the pits of Lancashire, although not relating specifically to Wigan. Of the Wigan area, Mr. Kennedy wrote of the colliers... "who are, without exception, the most degraded and wretched class of beings which has ever fallen under my notice..."

*No. 64 — Henry Jones* (in his sixth year).
    "What time do you go to work in the morning?" — "I go down about four o'clock."
    "What work are you put to?" — "I am a thrutcher" (a tub-drawer).
    "What time do you come up?" — "I should come up at 12, but it is sometimes later..."
    "Do you stop for meals?" — "No, we stop for noan (none)..."

*No. 65 — James Jones,* aged 11 (who worked a six-hour shift, one week and an eight-hour shift, the next week: another 'thrutcher').

"Have you ever worked longer hours?" — "The longest time I ever worked was 10 hours; none of the children work longer."

"Do you stop to take your food?" — "No, we don't stop; we eat when we have time."

"What do you get for dinner?" — "I get butter-cakes for breakfast, I have nothing to drink, and butter-cakes for dinner, except on Sundays, then I have bacon and potatoes or meat; I have thick porridge and another butter-cake for supper."

"Are you ever beaten?" — "No, they don't thrash me."

"What is the height of the main road?" — "It is a yard high."

"What heights are the roads in the workings?" — "...20 to 23 inches."

"Then you will have to creep on your hands and feet?" — "Yes."

"What is the weight of the tubs?" — "We draw 2¼ cwt."

"Are the tubs on sledges or wheels?" — "On wheels; there are rails..."

"Do you use the belt and chain?" — "Yes, one pulls in front, with a belt and chain and one, sometimes two thrutchers behind."

"What distance do you bring the coals?" — "Sometimes 800 or 900 yards."

"Is the mine steep?" — "There is a rise of one yard in six."

(Then follows details of supervision, ill-health, accidents.)

*NO. 55 — William Cooper* aged seven years (part of testimony).

"Are there any women in the pit you work in?" — "There are about 20 wenches, drawers (thrutchers)."

"How are they dressed?" — "They are nigh naked, they wear trousers. They have no other clothes except loose shifts and trousers."

*No. 90 — Betty Harris,* aged 37 (part of testimony).

"...I was married at 23, and went into a colliery when I was married. I used to weave, when about 12 years old. I can neither read nor write. I am a drawer and work from 6 o'clock in the morning to 6 at night. I make sometimes 7s a week, sometimes not so much.

"I have two children, but they are too young to work. I worked at drawing, when I was in the family way. I know a woman who has gone home and washed herself, taken to her bed, been delivered of a child, and gone to work again under a week.

"I have a belt round my waist, and a chain passing between my legs, and I go on hands and feet. The road is very steep, and

we have to hold by a rope, (or) by anything we can catch hold of
...it is very hard work for a woman. This pit is very wet where I
work, and the water comes over our clog-tops always, and I have
seen it up to my thighs.

"It rains in at the roof, terribly: my clothes are wet almost
all day long ..."

As elsewhere, during the industrial revolution of the early 19th
century, almost intolerable hardship was the common lot for the
working class. Human degradation went hand-in-hand with commercial exploitation.

By the 1860s, coal production in the Wigan area was going
upwards to the highest ever achieved. It was another 60—70 years
before the decline set in. Now, apart from open-cast mining and one
or two drift mines, only a few collieries remain.

During the period of ministry of Mr. Wickham at St. Andrew's,
coal strikes were common. True, the unbelievably cruel treatment of
labour down the pits had ended. Gone were the times when the
'trappers' — usually children between five and eight years old — sat
for 12 to 18 hours a day, either in total darkness or by candle-stub
glimmer, pulling ventilating shutters — for 3s a week or less.

Parliamentary legislation and a system of inspectorate, brought in
by the 1850 Act of Parliament, had wiped out the practice of men
and women working, virtually naked, side by side at the coal face,
along with all the other abuses that had reduced human beings to
little more than animals. Together with the 1842 'Employment of
Women and Children in Mines' Act, which did away with the
employment underground of all females, and of boys under 10 years
old, unforewarned visits by inspectors gradually stamped out the
conditions about which the social reformers had for long campaigned;
and encouraged a more humane attitude towards workers. Even so,
conditions down the pits were still grim and dangerous. During the
19th century, in the Wigan area alone, there were 829 recorded
deaths from explosions and other pit accidents; probably tens of
thousands of colliery workers received bad injuries; and very many
more had their health ruined by the working conditions and
accompanying health hazards.

Equally grim were the conditions in which the colliers and their
families lived. In 1844, the Commissioners for the Mines reported of
typical miners' cottages, "They are hovels rather than cottages,
having nothing but a ground floor; some consist of one, others of two
rooms, from 10 to 14 feet square each. Many of the older ones have
no ceiling; vacancies in the roof let in the wind and rain, and the
floor is damp, being often a little more than the natural ground."

Not a lot had changed, nearly 70 years later. An ex-collier recalling living conditions near Wallgate, Wigan, said... "In some of these back-to-back houses, there was only one room up and one room down; they had no gas and used to have to burn an oil lamp or candles... we were lucky, we lived in a two up and two down... we did have gas". And, of the Harrison Street 'back-to-backs'... "Now, in these houses, what 'slops' they would have, they had to empty, and as they lived in the front part of the house, they would have to come through the front with the slops to get to the street and down the entry into the toilet there. They were old middens, just an old tub with a seat cover."

Mr. Wickham's surviving daughters still remember such poor dwellings in the parish, candle-lit or gas-lit, with their primitive sanitation and washing facilities.

So the colliers had little to lose by striking. They were already living on the edge of, if not already in, dire poverty; and faced death, crippling injury, or ruined health daily. They also knew that, in the event of a strike, charity in some form would provide a degree of relief.

There had already been strikes in the early 1890s, and the situation came to a head in July 1893, when the owners asked for a 25 per cent reduction in pay on the increase in wages since 1888. This was equivalent to a cut in wages of nearly one-fifth — the man earning £1 a week was being asked to accept about 16s. The colliers refused, and struck. Through the rest of the summer and into the autumn the strike went on. A central relief committee was set up and, among other measures, 'soup kitchens' established. Along with the Chief Constable's Dept., St. Andrew's Church, the Primitive Methodists, and a Wigan firm, Wanklyn & McKay, set up kitchens. The St. Andrew's kitchen was providing one good meal a day for about 350 children from needy families. In the October issue of the parish magazine, Mr. Wickham recorded that each needy family was receiving four loaves of bread, 2 oz. tea and 'some pounds' of potatoes each week. He also organised entertainment for the colliers and their wives in the parish, in an endeavour to provide some light relief from the misery. This took the form of lantern shows; and a kind benefactor provided free tobacco for the men. The shows were well attended and, obviously, much enjoyed.

By November, the relief situation was very serious. The Vicar wrote in the magazine:

"The strike still drags on its weary way, and there is no immediate prospect of its termination. But the relief seems to be coming to an end. The Vicar has just received an intimation from the Central Committee that he must not expect any further subscriptions

'Miner setting a prop.' Note the effect of 'flash' on the coal-face (flower-head effect), and on one eye. Douglas Bank Colliery, 1891. (L.S.)

'St. Andrew's Soup Kitchen: Mr. Haworth serving.' The 1893 Coal Strike. (O.G.P.)

'Drawer pushing tub', to main road, where mechanical haulage took over, 1891. (Damaged L.S.)

'Collier under-cutting and boy drilling.' Undercutting gave room for the coal to 'blow', preventing it from shooting back, off coalface. Boy is drilling a hole for the shot, 1891. (L.S.)

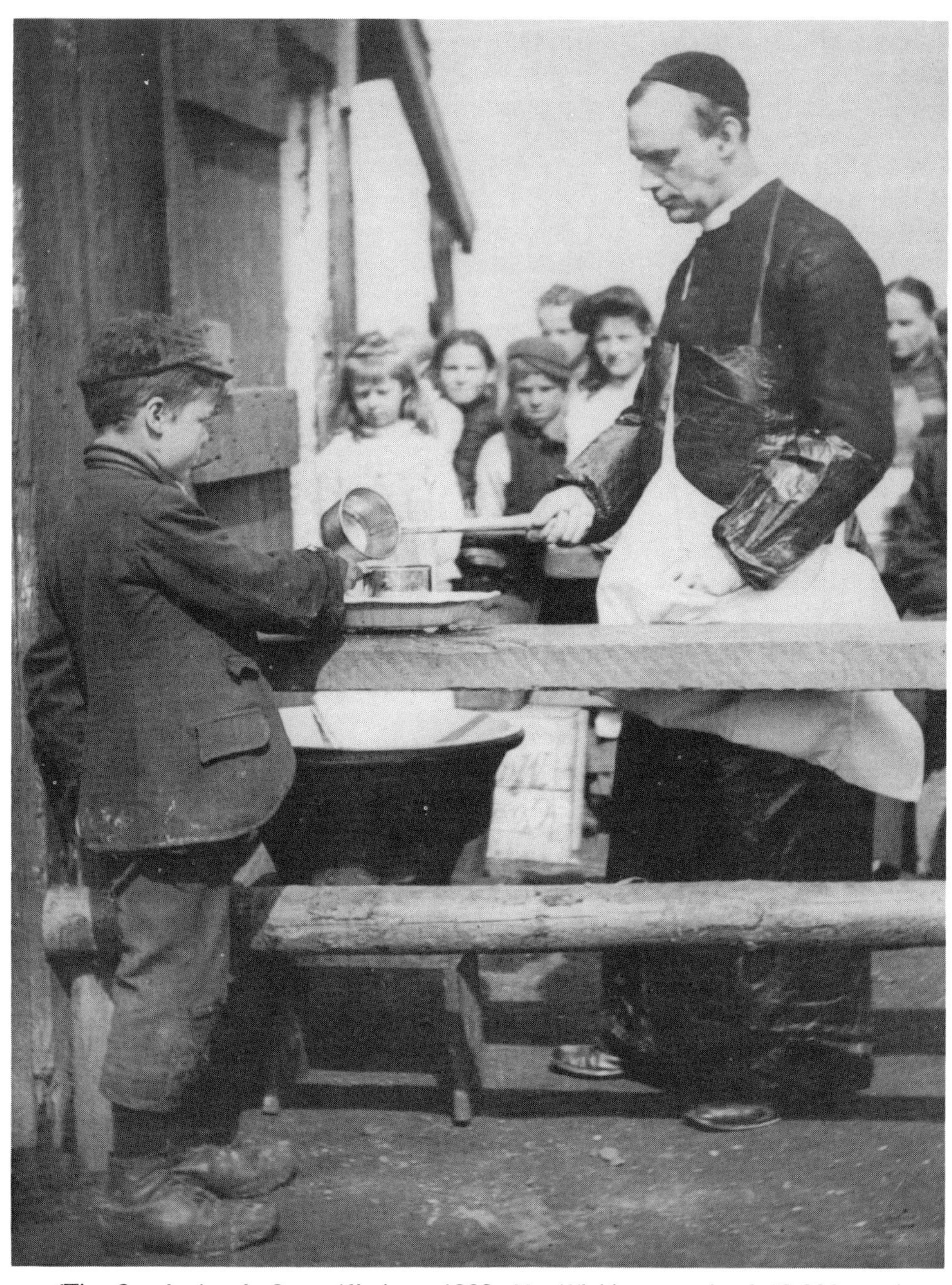

'The St. Andrew's Soup Kitchen, 1893, Mr. Wickham serving.' 18,000 meals were served, during the four-month strike. (O.G.P.)

'Collier entering cage': Douglas Bank Colliery, 1891. (L.S.)
'Cage arriving at bottom', 1891. (Badly-marked L.S.)

'Collier washing in kitchen', 1891. (L.S.)
'Collier taking his ease', 1891. (L.S.)

towards the Soup Kitchen, which will have to be closed, since the other subscriptions have all been withdrawn.

"Since the Soup Kitchen was opened on August 25th, about 17,000 dinners have been served from it. The Vicar has also very nearly exhausted all the available funds for the relief of the sick and poor, so that it will be quite out of his power to do more than give some small relief in the worst cases of sickness.

"Whoever is responsible for the continuance of the strike will have something to answer for. The prospect is, indeed, gloomy as winter comes nearer, and relief diminishes every day; and as the strain on people is greater.

"We can only say 'God help us'."

Widespread appeals for help, on behalf of the St. Andrew's Church effort, had brought some response. The Vicar acknowledged specifically £5 from the Editor of the 'Daily Chronicle' (this provided enough soup for three days), and a parcel of clothing from the Lancashire Needlework Guild. By this time, about 18,000 dinners had been served from the kitchen.

The coal strike ended on November 17th; and the December issue of the parish magazine carried a long article, asking 'Who has won?' It was a masterly assessment of the dispute and its 'ripple' effect by Mr. Wickham — and a full-blooded condemnation of the all-round futility of strikes.

"When we heard, on Friday, November 17th, that the dreadful 16 weeks' strike was over, our first feeling was one of deep thankfulness. On the following Sunday evening, the congregation in Church sang the 'Doxology' immediately after the sermon, as an act of special thanksgiving.

"Now that the strike is over, we may well look back upon it and speak of it without being suspected of bias or of taking sides. Let us consider the gains and losses of both sides, and the losses of the public generally, and then calmly ask the question: 'Was the strike right?'

"Who has won? Some say the masters, others the men. Is not the truer reply this — Both have lost.

"The masters have lost, clearly. They demanded a reduction, and after a 16 weeks' struggle, the men have gone [back] to work on the old terms. The masters must also have lost very heavily in £. s. d. We cannot tell what their losses have been.

"To those who had no stocks of coal, the strike must have meant nothing but loss. Those who had stocks had a chance of recouping their losses. But here we must remember that we may easily be very unfair to the masters. We must not forget that a rook of coal represents so much capital lying idle. It has been thrice paid for — to the men who have won the coal, to the royalty owners, and to the capital account. It has had to be put down and it has to be taken up, and there is depreciation.

"It has been estimated that all this represents quite 4s a ton, so that coal sold straight from the pit at a fair profit, at, say, 10s a ton, if sold from the rook after lying there for some time, has to be sold at 14s a ton, to enable the mine owner to make the same profit.

"If this be properly considered, we shall at once see that the profits of coal-owners, even on their coal rooks, are not so enormous as they are generally supposed to be. Making all possible allowances, we shall be safely within the truth if we say that coal-owners, as a body, have lost heavily by this strike.

"The masters, then, have lost. Have the men won? We are told that they have, but have they? Let us see.

"On July 29th they ceased work, rather than submit to the masters' demand for a reduction. The demand was for 25 per cent on the increase of wages since 1888, i.e. for about 18 or 19 per cent on their whole wage.

"Now, suppose they had at once submitted to this demand, the man who was earning £1 a week, instead of getting £50 a year would have earned £40. But, when the reduction was demanded, arbitration was offered. Arbitration means bargaining, and the man who offers to bargain is clearly prepared to take less than he originally asks.

"Consequently, no one will deny that, if the men had accepted arbitration, they would probably have got off with considerably less than the demand originally made. But, if there had been no arbitration — simply submission — we have seen that the man earning £1 a week would have earned £40 instead of £50.

"How will it be now? Sixteen weeks' wages (in some cases more than this) have been lost — i.e. the man earning £1 a week will earn £34 instead of £50. Is this much of a victory? It is much like the victory won by a man who should fight rather than part with his little finger, and who should, in the end, lose his thumb and forefinger instead.

"But then, it may be said the men were fighting not only against a reduction, but specially for the principle of a 'living wage'. Suppose it was so, where in terms of settlement signed by master and man, as published in the papers, is there to be found any concession on this principle? And without this, what is the proposed Board of Conciliation and its Independent Chairman but 'arbitration' under a different name?

"Where, then, is the men's victory? Their losses are evident, and they have been terrible. It will take many a long month to get over even some of these losses; some never can be got over. Money has been lost in abundance. Bad blood has been stirred, hard words have been spoken, and, sometimes, hard blows hit (though the behaviour of the men generally has been excellent).

"Men and women and children have been for weeks paupers, and in too many cases have acquired, for the first time in their lives, the pauper spirit.

"Many other evils may be added to these mentioned and, look at the thing from whatever point we will, it seems to us that the men, so far from winning a splendid victory, have suffered a terrible defeat.

"So far, we have spoken only of masters and men. There are others to be considered, in a matter of this sort; and neither masters nor men have any right to be selfish. The general public have a right to be considered, as well. Both masters and men have lost heavily, but the general public have lost, too — and in some cases have lost almost as heavily as the combatants themselves.

"This is so with the Ironworker. Their case is peculiarly hard. They have a sliding scale, and with bad trade their wages went down. With reviving trade, their wages were rising and, suddenly, through no fault of their own, they are thrown out of work and for many weeks have to starve.

"Then, think of the Shopkeepers, Owners of Cottage Houses (many of them working men themselves), Mill Hands, Builders, Brickmakers, and other tradesmen. Think of what the strike has meant to them.

"Think of what it has meant to the School Managers. Where are we going to find the £17 or so which we have lost in school pence alone, at St. Andrew's? 'Oh!, someone will give it to you'. Will they?

"There is something else to be borne in mind, and that is this, that for 16 weeks many thousands of pounds have been given to keep starving people alive, whilst at the same time the price of coal has been unusually high. All this has greatly reduced the power of people to give to churches and schools and hospitals; and all these good works must suffer, in consequence, because it has been often stated and proved that in England, in one year, there is only a certain amount given away in 'charity', and if it goes in one direction it does not go in another.

"Thus, everyone has been beaten and wounded in this most unhappy coal war. Who caused it? We will not attempt to decide this question. We will only say this, that whoever began the strife, and whoever continued it — it has been brutal work. The Home Secretary's words, spoken early in the conflict, have been fully justified.

"Whatever the merits of the case on either side, at the outset, the means taken to decide it have been most unworthy of a Christian or even of a civilised country. This terrible and unexampled strike has been surely enough to convince any thoughtful person that a 'strike' is a way of settling a dispute of which both sides ought thoroughly to be ashamed. Nothing parallel to it is allowed in ordinary life.

"If A and B have a quarrel, they are not allowed to fight it out with brickbats and pistols, in the open street... for fear lest they might injure each other, and at the same time injure the bystanders and the surrounding houses. They are stopped immediately, if they begin to fight. They have to go before a magistrate — in a word — to submit to arbitration.

"Why should it be otherwise, on a larger scale? Of course, the arbitration must be on a basis fair to both parties; but surely it will be possible, with a little mutual forbearance, to arrange this.

"Masters and men have been fighting it out, almost to the death, during the past 16 weeks; and the general public have been hit and hurt on all sides. This ought not to be possible in Christian England, at the close of the 19th century.

"But, if it is in the future to be avoided, both masters and men will have to be less selfish — content to give as well as to take, looking upon each other not as natural enemies, but as men in the same boat; and putting the best construction on each other's doings.

"May God heal all our wounds, and pour out upon us the Spirit of Peace."

Truly enough, the consequences of the strike began to make themselves felt. The payment of school pence for the year fell from £43 to £26 — a serious deficit. The Church income from offertory was down, and the Sunday School missionary boxes produced less than was anticipated. And the St. Andrew's Church charitable resources had been drained almost dry.

In the January 1894 issue of the magazine, the Vicar referred to the things that needed doing urgently — and expressed the hope that enough money would come in "to enable us to live on a little longer, in a hand-to-mouth way".

It was not a very happy New Year for Wigan St. Andrew's — or for many of its poor parishioners!

# Chapter 10

## *THE ST. ANDREW'S PARISH MAGAZINE*

In May 1879, Mr. Wickham launched the parish magazine. Introducing it, he said, "A Parish Magazine is a very useful piece of parish machinery. We make the experiment of starting one . . . we must sell at least 100 each month . . . the price is 1d, ready money . . . let us all try to keep this little ship afloat."

It was to become accountancy book, agony column, begging letter, a sort of 'readers' digest', home doctor; and the medium through which the Vicar spoke to the parish on matters of local, diocesan, national, and international importance. So we read:

*September 1882*

How many teetotallers are there, in the parish? The Vicar will soon want to know, and the more he finds, the better he will like it.

*February 1883*

The young men's Mutual Improvement Society is doing very well . . . papers have been read by Mr. Lumsden on 'The wonders of pond life', by Mr. Haworth on 'Wonders of the deep' and by the Vicar on Mr. Darwin's book on earthworms. One evening was devoted to the microscope.

*September 1883*

What is the good of going to church on a weekday morning? The congregation is so very small . . . I can do as well at home.

No, my friend, you cannot, I am bold to say . . . an older writer once said that two people praying together are like two pieces of coal, which burn better when they are close together than when they are apart.

*November 1883* (Regarding the Men's Mutual Improvement Society).

It should be borne in mind that there is no necessary connection between this society and St. Andrew's Church; and that men of any religious views, or none at all, may join it. The object is . . . to provide amusement and instruction for members during the winter months.

The subscription is 1d per fortnight.

and (*January 1884*)

...it is proposed to turn the Society into an Ambulance Class for some time. This will probably be most useful.

## SCARLET FEVER

*June 1884*

In consequence of the prevalence of Scarlet Fever in the Borough, the Sanitary Authority have issued a notice to the managers of the different schools, ordering them to close...for five weeks. St. Andrew's School will accordingly be closed until further notice. (Then follows general advice about the care of children with the disease, disinfection of bedding, etc.)

...and, *July 1884*

The Sanitary Authorities have ordered the Borough schools to be kept closed for another fortnight.

...and, *August 1884*

Another order has been sent to us to keep them [the schools] closed for four more weeks.

## EASTER

*May 1885*

We are glad that so many performed their Easter duty this year, but we are by no means satisfied when we think of the number who did not. WHY DID THEY NOT? Some few were unable. But most of those who did not come might have come had they so chosen. The fact was they did not choose. WHY NOT? Ah!

If they will deal honestly with themselves and search out the answer to that question, and abide by the decision of their own conscience, it will be well with them. Why should any poor, weak, sinful soul refuse to come to its dear Saviour?, its Bible, its Prayer-book, its Bishop, its Priest, its best friends — all urge it to come. But it chooses to stay away. Poor soul! Awful choice!

*July 1885*

The Mayoress, Mrs. Park, has sent us for signature a Petition to the Town Council, asking that the Pleasure Fair may be abolished on the ground that the fairs are a source of much grievous immorality, and are a most serious injury to the trade of the town and district, and they also largely interfere with public convenience and general industry...we hope many in St. Andrew's Parish will sign, for it says not one word more about fairs than is strictly true, and the wonder is they have not been done away with, here, as they have in many other places.

(A writer dealing with Victorian entertainment in the cotton towns of Lancashire wrote of the peep shows, freak exhibitions, and stalls "where there were girls exposing themselves to the public gaze, for money"...and George Sanger, writing of Stalybridge Wakes in 1850 said, "The Wakes were very rough affairs in those days, the Lancashire lads and lasses making holiday at them in the wildest possible fashion. The clog was their weapon, and they considered there was nothing unmanly in kicking and biting to death — for they would use their teeth like dogs..."

Writing of an attack on a stall-owner, he went on..."from our position on the platform, we could see the poor fellow's body with the heavy clogs battered into it as though it were a stuffed sack, instead of a human being".)


*August 1885* (on going to church on a hot day)

Writing of the Dedication Day service, the Vicar commented, "Sunday was a very hot day, although the ventilation of the church was excellent, the thermometer stood at 70°C. But the Vicar's study was just as hot, and probably the kitchens of the cottages in the parish were a good deal hotter, on account of the fire. Therefore, the people who stayed away to avoid the heat could not have gained very much more than the fish who hopped out of the frying pan, into the fire.

"Why do people feel the heat or cold much more in church than in other places? How much has fancy to do with it?

"In a certain church, ladies were continually fainting, and being tenderly assisted from church by the gentlemen who were sitting near them. The thing at last became a nuisance...and the Church-wardens were determined to stop it; and gave it out that all ladies who fainted in future would be forthwith placed under the pump, bonnets and all.

"After this, the ventilation was found to be excellent, and no one fainted. When people feel the heat or cold excessively in church, it is often (though not always) a sign that they are not attending to the service as much as they ought to be..."


*June 1887* (On sickness, visiting, and public charity).
Dear People,

There are several subjects on which I wish to address you.

First, with respect to sickness. When a person falls seriously ill, his friends immediately send for the *medical man*...Now the Parish Priest should be treated in exactly the same way as the Doctor...if he is worth having, he is worth fetching — and, if he is worth fetching, he is worth fetching in good time.

Just a word on another subject. I was taken to task, the other day, for not having visited an old person who had been resident in the parish for some time. I replied "You must blame yourself, not me...until last Sunday, I did not know of her existence".

No one ever thinks of blaming a doctor for not visiting an invalid of whose sickness he knows nothing...Sometimes, to judge by the excuses they make, people seem to give their parish priest credit for being a bigger fool than ordinary. At other times, they treat him as though he were gifted with a Divine Omniscience: knowing everything without being told. They are in error both ways.

There is yet one more subject. I have had at various times entrusted to me for distribution, tickets for the Mayor's Feasts, and also Clothing Tickets and Public Charity money. They are entrusted to me as being likely, as parish priest, to be better acquainted with people's circumstances than an outsider.

They are not given to me to give to *Churchpeople.* Neither have churchpeople more claim to them than those who are not churchpeople. I am afraid some of you have not quite understood this. I hope you will understand it, now.

I have never made, and I never shall make any distinction in my distribution of such things. I have always striven and shall strive to be absolutely impartial. I can fearlessly say I have always been so, to the best of my knowledge. I have never asked and never shall ask whether a person is a nominal Churchman or a real one — a Papist or Protestant, Dissenter, or Infidel..."

*July 1887*

THE STRANGE DEATH IN SCHOLES (from the 'Wigan Observer')

Re-publication, in the parish magazine, of the inquest on a fit man who died of asphyxia through sleeping in an overcrowded bedroom. (There were 11 people sleeping in two rooms, in the house.)

The Vicar's comment followed: "Overcrowding in a bedroom is very common in houses in this parish and elsewhere...It is morally very injurious and injurious to health. In Michael Carney's case...he was in good health, and went to bed well. Next day, he was dead — poisoned. Poisoned by carbonic acid gas — a deadly poison.

"We breath in pure fresh air; we breath out carbonic acid gas. Each of us, awake or asleep, needs a certain space of air in which to breathe. If we have less than this, we breathe in again the carbonic acid gas we have previously breathed out..."

The Vicar goes on to give simple advice on home ventilation, concluding, "We cannot neglect the laws of health and expect to get off scot free".

*March 1890*
### TO THOSE WHO GAVE THE VICAR HIS CASSOCK
My dear friends,

I have been taken to task by some of my friends ... for receiving your kind present rather ungraciously ... Now what one person thinks, another may think ... and, therefore, I write you a few words on the subject. Believe me, I am deeply grateful to you for the kind feeling — the too kind feeling — that prompted the gift. I cannot value that too highly. Nevertheless, if you had consulted me beforehand, I should have begged you not to make me a present, because I happen to have a strong dislike to personal presents to myself ....

I daresay this is one of my infirmities — like rheumatism, or a cold in the head. I don't know that I could defend the dislike in any rational or Christian way ... and moreover, of all presents, I most dislike those which take the shape of public testimonials from his people to their parish priest ... Such testimonials often are — which I am sure yours was not — very unreal and deceptive.

They are often wrung from many unwilling givers, who no more love the parson than they do the parson's cat, but who do not like — or perhaps dare — to refuse ... Please do not think ill of me if I add *'don't do it again'* ... I hope I shall wear the cassock for many years, in your service, and I have ordered that, together with the surplice in which I was ordained, it shall serve me for my shroud.

Your faithful servant in Christ,<br>
W. A. Wickham.

*October 1890*
### A WORKING MAN: AND GIVING TO GOD
A friend of mine, a working chap, as his lingo will show you (writes C.W.M.), told me once: "When me and my wife gotten wed, we sattled it between oursens that whattiver comed, God wore to have His share ov t'wage. And, as sure as Saturday neet comed, she wod lift it on t'shelf. Weel, when I wor ill and out ov wark we was badly off, but somehow we allus had summat to put on t'shelf.

"When I gotten weel, ther' was no wark for me, and I thowt we sud have pined but we didn't. An' I got a job and went home and me and my missus we had a reet jollification, when wage neet comed. 'Well' says I, and looks at her ... een says I 'I think lass we ought to raise His wage an' all. And we put 2s 6d on t'shelf, and have nivver put less sin'.''

*December 1890*

During Advent, there will be a Lantern Service in the church, each Monday evening at 7.30 p.m. We hope for a good attendance; the church will be well warmed. No books will be used, so those that cannot read should come. Old clothes will do as well as better ones, because the church will only be dimly lighted, and no one will be able to see their neighbour's clothes. Deaf people will at any rate be able to see the pictures. Come yourself, and try to bring with you some neighbour who is not in the habit of coming to church.

*November 1891* (Announcement of another Lantern Show)

...We hope all our old workers will be so kind as to try once more to sell plenty of tickets. ...We do not, however, want any babies and we have decided to charge a baby £5 for admission. We hope the price will prove prohibitive. Last time, a baby made itself heard much better than the lecturer...and the baby was not happy, either.

*July 1894*

The Vicar published in the May magazine a List of Wants.

Some of his friends have rather laughed at him...for asking so much, at once.

In November 1888, he published a similar list, and was similarly laughed at. Since then he has received of the things asked, the following: Money to pay off the organ debt; nearly £1600 for the new schools; £400 more for the Vicarage; money to pay for the reredos paintings; a handsome banner; the white silk pulpit desk hanging; the pictures of the chancel screen and money to paint and improve it (twice as much as was asked for); money for the carving of the pillars, and for the oak work behind the font and by the sides of the organ front.

Thus, encouraged by past experience, the Vicar issued the list of wants, in May, and already several have been supplied.

*May 1897*

### DIALOGUE BETWEEN THE PARSON AND A DEAF PARISHIONER

Parishioner: "Why, I thought you were off."

Parson: "No, I go the week after next. But it surely would not make any difference to you, If I were to go for ever."

Parishioner: "How do you make that out?"

Parson: "You never come near me."

Parishioner: "Well, you see I am deficient here" (touching his ear).

Parson: "I once knew an old man who was as deaf as a post, and he never missed coming every Sunday."

Parishioner: "And what good did that do him?"

Parson: "He did his duty and worshipped God."

Parishioner: "I do that every night of my life."

Parson: "You should do more than that. You should worship him in church, because you are not only an individual Christian, but also a member of the Church — the Body of Christ."

It is quite as much the duty of the deaf as of those who can hear, to join in public worship. It is also the duty of the blind and lame. Public worship is a duty for all, and cannot be neglected without sin.

*July 1897* (On the Choir Treat)

Either one of two things is certain: the choir boys have been bad beggars, or those from whom they have begged have been bad givers. Anyway, the result is sad, for under £3 is in hand...

[Mr. W. H. Morgans, a parishioner, was born in 1898, "When coal was 6d a cwt", he told me. He joined the St. Andrew's Choir when 10 years old and, reminiscing on the annual Choir Treat, said, "We choir boys had to tout for public support, each boy being allotted a definite area — in my case, the street in which I lived. I went to the home of a sidesman and felt sure of his support, but his wife had other ideas. 'No. I could do with someone getting up a treat for me'.

"Another neighbour, disturbed at his toilet, came to the door, lather on face and razor in hand. His Sweeney-Todd-like approach 'If tha doesn't be off, I'll slit thi' gizzard'."]

*December 1901* (Typhoid fever)

This parish has suffered heavily, of late, from typhoid fever. During the past few months, there have been at least 16 cases...We have had more than our share of typhoid for some years past, and the wonder is that we have not had more of it. For beyond the Douglas Bank Colliery offices there is no main sewer. Moreover, the sanitary arrangements of many of the older houses are almost as bad as they can be....

No one seems to stir effectively in the matter, and so we go on. Many innocent persons have to suffer, and some precious lives are lost. We sometimes wonder whether our ward representatives on the Town Council know the state of things.

It would perhaps quicken their interest and strengthen their hands, if someone were to send them (and also the Medical Officer of Health) a list of those who have suffered from typhoid, during the last 10 years, and of those who have died.

*April 1903* (Re the granting of a licence to a public house to be built just outside the parish boundary)

The Vicar dealt with this, at length. At the opening of the Sessions, the then Mayor of Wigan had expressed the opinion of the magistrates that 'the number of Public Houses in their district exceeds the legitimate requirements'. Nevertheless, the licence was granted.

The Vicar opposed it on the grounds that, of the 87 houses to be considered, and which had been canvassed by two trustworthy men, only two desired a Public House, 12 were neutral or absent and 73 were against it. This fact had been sworn to, and made a legal fact.

Quoting from the magazine: "The learned counsel on the other side [F. E. Smith, later to become Lord Chancellor] had every opportunity of upsetting the testimony of the witness. He made no attempt to do so, beyond asking a sapient question which, as the Vicar immediately showed, was equivalent to a suggestion that the St. Andrew's people were fools.

"Hence, we may take it that 84% of the householders were strongly opposed to this licence...and yet the Justices granted it; and that too, in the face of their admirable statement quoted above!

"How much easier it is to preach than to practice!"

(It is relevant to relate here that, earlier, Mr. Wickham was the owner of a Staffordshire bull terrier. The Vicar was in dispute with another public house over the sale of drink. What transpired, we do not know. But one of the daughters recalls the story — and of a message being received at the Vicarage, from the public house, requesting that someone go and collect the dog, which was sitting outside the 'pub' door, and would neither let customers in nor out.)

*January 1907*

### CARE FOR AGED PARENTS

The neglect of aged parents, which is so common amongst us, is indeed sad and shameful. The Fifth Commandment binds us, as long as our parents are alive, and we cannot neglect them, without sin. Moreover, if we neglect our parents, what can we expect for ourselves, when our turn comes to be old.

*July 1907*

### SIDESMEN'S STAVES

It was agreed at the last two Vestry Meetings that the sidesmen on duty should sit in the aisles, and keep their eyes on the good [Vicar's humour] boys who sit there. As a little reminder of the duty, we have lately placed four stout oaken staves at the end of four seats. They are not intended for use, except as a reminder....

*May 1908*

With regard to the CHURCH DRAUGHT, we transcribe the following words from a book by the late Dr. John Watson, a Presbyterian Minister in Liverpool... "We touch at this point the inexhaustible question of draughts, and must leave it alone, with the following observations, for the comfort of the Ministry: That there never has been any church yet, without a draught; that is the only reason why certain people do not attend with regularity; that a draught of ten horsepower would not keep them from a theatre or a reception; that the Officers of the Church will receive fifty suggestions a year how to cure the draught, but that the genuine Church Draught cannot be cured by physical expedients; that, in short, it is a device of the Prince of Power in the air, as any man with Celtic blood in his veins knows.''

There we must leave it. But we cannot admit that the St. Andrew's Church draught is worse than other church draughts.

*October 1913*

## A COOMFERT

In the 'Wigan Observer' of September 20th, there is an account of an inquest on a child, held at Platt Bridge. The mother had given a child of 5 weeks old two eggspoonsful of a mixture of laudanum [opium tincture] and aniseed, which she had heard from an 11-year-old girl that it was used to keep babies quiet. It was labelled 'Laudanum. Poison. Dangerous to Children'...the doctor told the Coroner that 2 or 3 drops would be fatal for a child of that age.

It came out at the inquest that these injurious drugs were largely sold by a woman in the neighbourhood. Said the Coroner, ''The absolute ignorance that is walking about is appalling''...and that it was a lamentable thing that infant life should be endangered in this way.

Mr. Wickham wrote, ''The Vicar is grateful to the coroner for speaking out thus...children are an heritage and a gift which cometh from the Lord, and they ought to be taken the greatest care of. 'Soothing Syrups' and 'Comforters' are both thoroughly bad for them. If a child cries much, it is a sign that a doctor ought to see it, or else that it is being too much indulged or improperly fed''.

*September 1914*

## THE WAR

We cannot do better than print some of the recent words of Mr. Robert Blatchford, the well-known Socialist. ''We are at war. We are committed to a war that will be desperate and terrible in its action, and its results appalling. And here are young men flirting, riding, swimming — 'fleeting' the hours away''.

Every one of those merry, careless men ought to have a rifle on his shoulder. Every one of those happy girls ought to be at work, preparing for the hardest trial that ever came upon the British nation.

This is no time for play. This is a time of war. Do the British people realise yet, why we are at war? And what war means to all of us?... we are not fighting because we want to fight, but because we must...

Mr. Wickham goes on to tell his parishioners of militant Germany's aims, and of the sacrifices that have to be made. Then offers advice to young unmarried men, and to those who cannot leave home.

Giving a list of all who have gone to war, from the parish, he says, "It is easy enough to shout 'Britons never shall be slaves', but if they will not get ready to fight, they may find themselves 'slaves' before they know where they are".

*July 1915*

## THE BRITISH EMPIRE

It is the most wonderful thing that the world has ever known, and the most beneficient. It has grown gradually, and has been acquired in various ways. But we must never forget that God gave it to us. We form part of it... we ought, therefore, to be proud of it, to be thankful for it, and to love it.

Patriotism, i.e. Love of one's Country, is a duty. True (as opposed to false) patriotism shows itself in self-sacrifice for the Country's sake... (The Vicar ends with the words of 'Land of Hope and Glory'.)

Mr. Wickham concluded his stewardship of the St. Andrew's parish magazine (which he had kept going for 37½ years) with (September 1916) a long article on his leaving, and his new parish; (October, 1916) a full description of all the church furnishings, with much architectural and ecclesiastical amplification and the story of the building of St. Andrew's Church; and (December 1916) his farewell letter to his parishioners, reviewing his 38 years of ministry in Wigan.

Chapter **11**

## *FAMILY LIFE AT WIGAN*

At the funeral service for my old friend, Harry Godwin, we sang his favourite hymn: 'All Things Bright and Beautiful' — a child's hymn, someone thought. But Harry had been born into Victorian England, and was brought up knowing that

'The rich man in his castle, the poor man at his gate
God made them, high or lowly, and order'd their estate'.

Mr. Wickham recognised it, too. Why else the laying of the foundation stone for St. Andrew's Church by four people, each representing one of the recognised 'social classes' of the day? To him, it was the Christian stewardship of their 'estate' that mattered.

So, at the vicarage, the life of the Wickham children was ordered to their estate, as children of a man of vocation.

The Wickhams moved in the the new vicarage in January 1897, with Myrtle (nearly four), Bernard (two) and Cicely (11 months). It was a building described by the architect to the Ecclesiastical Commissioners as "a good, plain, substantial house with no nonsense about it". On January 12th, Mr. and Mrs. Wickham gave a 'house-warming' party for 55 church-workers and officials.

Apart from church-going, the young family had no contact with the ordinary children of the parish ('for fear of us picking up the Lancashire dialect', said one of the daughters). Perhaps, also, for fear of them contracting scarlet fever, tuberculosis, or other mortal illness that particularly plagued the parish.

Monica Wickham was once told by her father, "Monica, if you don't work harder at school (St. Elphin's School, for the daughters of clergymen) I'll take you away and send you to school with the Johnson girl (who, at that time, was going to Wigan High School).

Quoting from Mr. W. Morgans again: "Mr. W. had several daughters, who seemed remote from us lads; his son, whom we rarely saw, was an object of curiosity. He was studious-looking, bare-headed, and wore a uniform — white cravat, dark blue cassock, leather belt, shoes and yellow socks. Perhaps he was from a London School or College''. (This was a description of Bernard in Christ's Hospital uniform. He was dubbed 'yaller legs' by the local lads, who delighted in following him down the street, shouting it after him.)

And Mrs. Edna Cross (née Willgoose), whose grandparents helped to run the soup kitchen during the 1893 coal strike and whose father, 'Ted' Willgoose, a cabinet maker, made some beautiful pieces of church furnishing for St. Andrew's, told me (1980): "The girls used to sit on the vicarage wall, waving cheerfully by passers-by. And I can remember seeing them carrying home bags of nettles, for washing and then cooking, as a green vegetable.''

The Wickhams did not live superabundantly at the vicarage for Mr. Wickham's initial stipend of £150 per annum had only increased to £400 in the course of 38 years at St. Andrew's church. Some assistance came through Mrs. Wickham. who was well looked after by way of gifts from her family — with her brother, Alfred, often helping her financially.

Scrutiny of the photographs of the vicarage interior, for instance, reveals that much of what can be seen came from three specific sources: wedding-day presents, gifts from parishioners, and articles acquired by Mr. Wickham, and subsequently renovated, altered, or 'cannibalised' to make other articles.

On their wedding-day, the Wickham's received exactly 100 gifts (Monica made a list of them, years later), including a number of substantial pieces of furniture. At other times, several of his parishioner friends gave quite valuable pieces.

Mr. Wickham had a good eye for items, often abused and in very poor shape, with which something might be done. He began collecting bits of furniture whilst at Talke-o-the-Hill, buying from dealers, pawnbrokers, and people he met whilst on parish duties. Myrtle, his eldest daughter, eventually catalogued these and the record still remains. Examples:

*Over-mantel* picked up either in Wigan or Talke. This was concocted by my father from portions of a chest and a table. The second 'W' is the original letter. There was a key-hole next to it, and another letter on the other side of it. He had these removed and some oak inserted, on which he carved the remaining initials of his name, to give the 'W.A.W.'.

*Grandfather clock.* Given to my father by the daughter of the late Mr. Ormesher, sometime churchwarden of St. Andrew's. Was in a ruinous condition, and delivered to the backyard on a foggy day and left there, Cleaned and restored.

*'Noah's Ark.'* Obtained from a cottage in Marsh Green. It really is a court cupboard of unusual shape. The owner let father have it for the price of a new chest of drawers. The cottage children used to pretend it was a Noah's Ark, and 'take refuge' in it from the Flood.

*Oak chest on landing.* This had been used as a fodder chest and had been entirely neglected, various 'varmints' families being established inside of it; and the top of it off. Found by my father's mother at Mr. Ormesher's farm and purchased for 5s. Cleaned and restored.

Myrtle's list totals 35 items, of which some are mentioned, with the photographs. The vicarage truly was a museum of metamorphosis.

Mrs. Wickham made what family clothes she could. The girls dresses were plain — and all made from the same bolt of cloth, until it was used up; they were handed down from eldest to youngest. Mrs. Wickham was an excellent cook; and provided her family with good, wholesome food, in great variety — there were plenty of puddings, pies, junkets, etc. and home-made bread and preserves. Items such as flour were bought in bulk: the daughters recall the flour-barrel, and the big stone jar of honey. It was always Lancashire hot-pot on Sundays, prepared the day before.

Each day began with prayers, before breakfast. After breakfast, the children were taught by their mother, as she busied herself in the kitchen: reading, writing and arithmetic. They also had to do compositions, which their father set them and marked. They were also taken on walks by him, learning much of natural history. Then there was the daily walk with the current mother's help. Of them all, a Miss Pearce was remembered for her fierceness. Monica and Caroline recall having to walk in front of her, and getting prodded in the back with the ferrule of her umbrella for not walking straight-backed. They were taken on shopping trips to the market — a half-penny tram-ride; and once, they recall, on a visit to a waxworks exhibition.

On weekdays, from 3 p.m. to 6 p.m., Mr. and Mrs. Wickham went to visit the sick and others in need; the children worked for their pocket-money in the vicarage garden. Then came tea in the nursery; then down to be with their parents at their tea, at which time they were read to. After this, their mother read to them from a children's Bible, before supper and bed.

Saturday was sermon day, and no visitors allowed. Mr. Wickham paced his study, Titchums at his heels during the cat's lifetime. Some Saturdays, when the weather was good, the children would go with their father to Standish Woods. There they would play, whilst he sat and worked at his sermon, in the gamekeeper's hut which they called 'The Den'.

'The Vicarage Dining Room.' 'Noah's Ark' is to the left. On top, (centre) is Communion bread-wafer press. Overmantel was made from an old chest (see inscription T.G. 1661), bought from a dealer. Oak arm-chair came from a Cannock Chase cottage; Mr. Wickham had it repaired, cushioned and covered. 1897. (O.G.P.)

'The Vicarage Drawing Room.' Note Mr. Wickham's double-bass, some of his photographs, and the W.A.W. mantelpiece (see text). Cabinet on right comprises a chest, bed-posts, and a cabinet altered by local carpentry — typical 'Wickham' cannibalisation. Total cost — about £6. 1897. (O.G.P.)

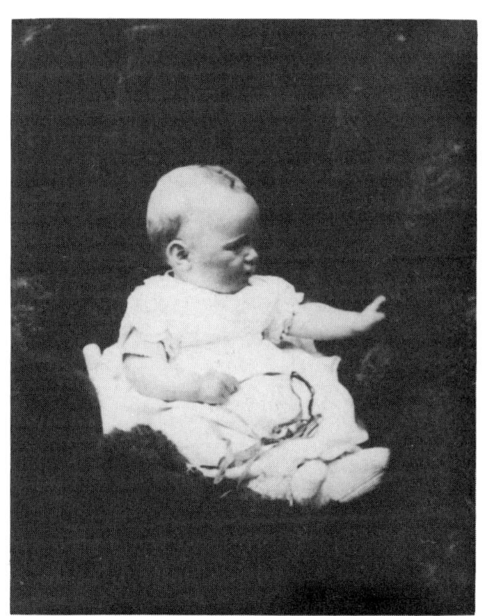

*'Bernard on rug', 1894. (O.G.P.)*
*'Bernard with foxglove.' (O.G.P.)*

*'Bernard in Christ's Hospital uniform', 1907. (O.G.P.)*
*'Lt. Bernard Wickham. M.C.', 1916. (O.G.P.)*

*'All five at the tent.' A 'fun' picture, in the vicarage garden. Sadly, too many sitters moved. L. to R. Caroline, Monica, Cicely, Bernard, Myrtle. (O.G.P.)*

 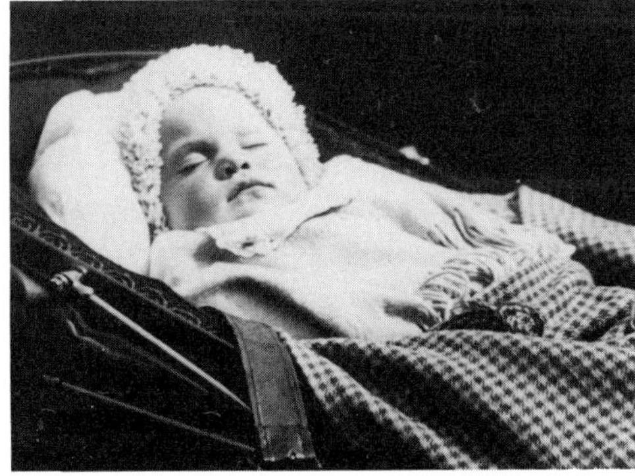

*'Bernard and Myrtle.' (O.G.P.)*

*'Myrtle asleep in pram.' (O.G.P.)*

'Bernard and Myrtle on rug.' (O.G.P.)

'Cicely in Vicarage doorway,' 1907. (O.G.P.)

'Mrs. Martha Peck' (Mrs. Wickham's mother). (O.G.P.)

On Sundays, the children were taken to Matins, sitting in the back pew with their mother, who took note of those present, as did the Vicar from the pulpit. On one occasion, Mr. Wickham decided that Bernard was not paying attention to the sermon, and challenged him to give the gist of it when back at the vicarage. To his acute embarrassment Bernard quoted it almost verbatim.

After Sunday lunch, the children had to learn the Collect for the day, and recite it to their mother. When they were older, they joined her at Evensong. They helped with church work, too. Every month, there were hundreds of parish magazines to be folded and put into envelopes. Missionary boxes had to be emptied, money counted, labels soaked off, and new ones put on.

At various times, apart from the mother's help, there was a woman who came in to do the washing (in a coal-fired copper, in the cellar); an odd-job man who carried coals, chopped wood, cleaned boots, etc.; and a maid.

Frank Colwell, who died in 1960, gave the Vicar and his family yeoman service in his youth. He had a busy time as boot-boy, for Mr. Wickham wore a different pair every day, being in receipt of a continuous legacy of boots and shoes, from deceased relatives and friends. Frank bought a shirt of Mr. Wickham's at a jumble sale and treasured it all his life, insisting that he be laid out in it when he died (which he was).

The maids have passed unremembered, except for a Norwegian who was at the vicarage when only Caroline, of the children, was still at home. Mr. and Mrs. Wickham went out one night, leaving her in the maid's care. They arrived back to find the maid, mentally deranged, rampaging around the vicarage yard, waving an axe. Caroline, to their great relief, was unharmed in bed.

Life was not altogether serious for the children. There were frequent visits to Liverpool, to see the progress being made in the building of the Lady Chapel of the new Cathedral, with Mr. Wickham taking photographs. Then, picnic outings to Ashurst Beacon and to Rivington Pike. As all became older, they had long walks together, often along the canal, to watch the boats being hauled through the locks by the fine, strong horses.

Annual holidays recalled particularly were those at Wreakes End, Coniston, in the Lake District; and at Holyhead, where they stayed at a farm with an earth-closet at the bottom of an orchard. "You took an apple as you went by, and ate it as you sat".

Mr. Wickham was a great walker; and the daughters' favourite recollection is of the two-day holiday during which the whole family walked about 20 miles. First: the train ride (probably to Garstang); then the walk through the Trough of Bowland, a wild, heather-and-gorse-covered moorland pass over the Forest of Bowland. Mrs. Wickham carried a spare pair of shoes round her neck. They stayed overnight at a farm: the children remember washing in the beck. Then on until hungry, thirsty and tired, they reached the outskirts of Clitheroe. Mr. Wickham bade Monica and Caroline to knock at a cottage door and say "Wickham of Wigan would like some tea, please". Impishly, they did so — and, to their delight, all were invited in and had a splendid tea in an old-world garden. Much refreshed, they went on and caught the train back to Wigan.

During the summer, they had a sort of makeshift tent in the vicarage garden, played the usual children's games — and got up to the usual children's pranks. Occasionally, some punishment had to be administered. Any child misbehaving, or telling lies had to go to the study to fetch the 'black elephant'; this was a paper-knife with an elephant-head handle. "Be snaped", said Mr. Wickham. Then, the offenders received some whacks on the hand from him — or a few slaps on the bottom, from their mother. This was followed by banishment to a bread-and-water tea.

Their education continued at home until they were aged between 8 and 10 years old. Then, one by one, they went off to boarding-school, leaving their 'hand-me-downs', their toys and dolls, their pets; and the close family environment.

Speaking of pets, mention must be made of one, Dick Richard 1st — a canary bought from a collier for 5s, as a birthday gift for Monica. The children used to dress it up in miniature doll's clothes, and sail it up and down the bath, in a pie-dish. On the day Monica went off to boarding-school for the first time, the canary died. The verdict of an autopsy was apoplexy — but Monica always believed it died of a broken heart.

So, eventually, Mr. Wickham was left to his increasing parochial and extra-parochial commitments and Mrs. Wickham to the running of her Mother's Meeting, her classes for pit brow lasses, and her assisting role in parish welfare and succour. The vicarage only came fully to life again when the children came home for holidays.

Chapter 12

*DUTIES AND DIVERSIONS*

In his farewell letter to his Wigan parishioners, in December 1916, Mr. Wickham wrote of the many extra-parochial tasks he had undertaken, during the 38 years of his ministry there.

He said, "A certain portion of my time has been given to Diocesan work. I joined the Committee of the Benefices Augumentation Fund in 1887, and during the past 11 years have been its Honorary Secretary; I was on the governing body of the Schools Association, and Hon. Secretary of the Wigan Rural Deanery Sub-Association, from 1897 to 1912. I was Convenor and Chairman of the Diocesan Records Committee from August 1909 to March 1910, when the report was presented.

"I am still on the General Cathedral Building Committee [Liverpool], the Cathedral Organisation Committee, the Bishop's Fund Organisation Committee, and the General Committee of the Diocesan Finance Association. For about 10 years, I was one of the Cathedral Lecturers giving, in that time, about 60 lectures, in the diocese and outside it.

"With the exception of this latter, for which I offered myself, all this diocesan work came to me unsought; I undertook it because it seemed plain duty. Of course, it necessitated the expenditure of much time and strength, and I mention it here because it seems necessary, in a review of my life with you. I do not think the parish was altogether the loser...."

Dealing first with his links with Liverpool: the Lord Bishop, making a special presentation to him a few weeks later, referred to the earnest and conscientous work he had carried out in the cause of religious education; to his keen interest in the building of the cathedral; and to his able and thoughtful lectures; also to his 11 years of hard work as Honorary Secretary of the Benefices Augmentation Fund. Mr. Wickham had shown a keen interest in the building of the Lady Chapel of Liverpool Cathedral. With his practical experience of raising a church at Wigan, coupled with all he had assimilated of church architecture and furnishings on his travels, he must have been a very valuable member of the Building Committee. When the Lady Chapel was consecrated in July 1910, it was Mr. Wickham who, as 'Our Special Correspondent', wrote a substantial and informative report for 'The Guardian' (July 1st edition).

Many of the cathedral records were destroyed during the air-raids of the Second World War; there remains nothing written to link Mr. Wickham with the Lady Chapel. The Lord Bishop had no doubt of his worth to the diocese, for he said that it owed a deep debt of gratitude to him, and would never forget the work he had done.

Was it Mr. Wickham's reputation as an 'expert' that prompted the ladies of the Liverpool Cathedral Embroidery Association to invite him to address them, in 1908? And was it a justification of their excellent judgement, that his address was subsequently printed in brochure form 'By Request'?

Addressing the ladies, whose collective responsibility it was to work on the altar frontals and the hangings in the Sanctuary, he reminded them that they had asked for 'an authority' to speak to them. He added that he had only come because the term had been qualified to include anything remotely connected with their work. He said, quoting an old Spanish proverb, "Call me not an olive till you see me gathered".

That disposed of, he proceeded to give an historical discourse on altar table coverings and English women's church needle-work, going back to the 8th century. He then dwelt on the great Winwick altar carpet, and a rare altar frontal, dated A.D. 1470, which was in the parish church at Alveley, in Shropshire. He concluded. "If you remember that your work is being done especially for God, it will bring out all the best that is in you. The end will sanctify the means and, if the end of the work be the glory of God, the work itself will become a holy work, and even a means of sanctification. God will have much to say to you, in the quietude of your work for Him.

"Fra Angelico used to say that he who practised the art of painting (and it is at least true of embroidery) had need of quiet; and that he who does Christ's work should live with Christ ... there can be no better example for a Christian embroideress."

Mr. Wickham's work on the Wigan Schools Association and as Secretary of the Rural Deanery Sub Association involved a great deal of time; also, scrupulous fairness in the allocation of the voluntary aid grants, given by the Government of the day from 1896 onwards. He undertook it all with his customary thoroughness and impartiality.

That he coped with all these commitments outside the parish is a tribute to his exceptional physical and spiritual resources, for he was a far from fit man, nor was he a young man. In 1888, he had suffered rheumatic fever, and was off duty for some time. Later, he developed phlebitis — and, in 1900, he had a complete breakdown in health. He went abroad to recuperate, taking Mrs. Wickham with him, at the Bishop's insistence. Great kindness was shown to them by the Bishop and Mrs. Chavasse, who took in the two eldest of the children not away at boarding school, and cared for them along with their own family of seven children. Mr. Wickham was ill again in 1916, and off duty for a while. As he told his parishioners at the time, if he had a curate there were times when he would have stayed in bed instead of going about his duties.

It is all the more noteworthy, therefore, to find that apart from all his 'duties', and all his photography, he found time actively to pursue an ecclesiological interest of great intensity and objectivity.

His many photographs show his enthusiasm for the scientific and the artistic in the building, decorating, and furnishing of sacred places. His learned papers, presented to the Historic Society of Lancashire and Cheshire over the period 1907 to 1916, are stamped with the hallmark of expertise. The subject matter is studied and researched to the $n$th degree and conclusions are drawn fearlessly; nor does he spare those who have neglected their stewardship. At the same time, he makes recommendations for improving the care and appearance of these 'treasures', where appropriate.

In 1907, he presented his paper 'Pugin, and the Rebuilding of Winwick Chancel'. In 1908, 'Some Notes on Aughton' dealing with 12th century Aughton Church. (Even the name interests him: he tells us it was 'Acheton' in the Domesday Book, probably meaning 'Oak Homestead'; and that it is pronounced 'Aff'n', locally.) In 1909, he presented 'Some Notes on Billinge' (16th century Billinge Church). In 1910, 'Some Notes on Hindley Chappell' — built in the latter half of the 18th century.

Mr. Wickham's 1912 paper, 'Some Notes on Chapter Houses' is particularly substantial. The bound re-print of this transaction of the Society occupies 108 pages, with some of Mr. Wickham's and other photographs, and drawings. He offered this treatise as the first one in which, to the best of his knowledge, chapter houses had been dealt with as a separate subject; and the Appendix lists the main details of 128 chapter houses.

In 1914, he presented 'The Anglian Cross-head at Aughton, and other recent discoveries there'. Included in the 'credits' for photographs and drawings is the name of his son, Bernard. In 1915, he dealt with Cockersand Chapter House; Cockersand Abbey was founded c. 1190, for the Order of White Canons, who colonised it from Croxton, in Leicestershire. Prior to the building of the abbey, there had been a hermit's cell and a leper hospital there. The 13th century chapter house is all that remains.

Mr. Wickham is also known to have helped in the preparation of a paper 'The 15th century Angels Bearing Shields of Arms, from Aughton Church', by Philip Nelson, M.D., F.S.A., and following his detailed investigation at Aughton, he was confident that he had established the date of the north aisle. He submitted his notes to the architectural editor of the Victoria History of Lancashire, whose comment was "The notes are very good, and establish the date of the present north aisle beyond any reasonable doubt...after reading Mr. Wickham's notes, I have inserted his conclusions, with due acknowledgement, in the proofs".

In this paper Mr. Wickham included a rebuff to those responsible for the care of the church, saying, "I earnestly hope that, if any further 'restoration' is undertaken, it may be as conservative as possible...much of the interest of this interesting church has already been 'restored' away". Prior to his investigations, a Norman doorway had been made into the chancel aisle despite the fact that there was, in his view, no evidence of any original work of that period in that part of the church.

To one like myself, completely unacquainted with church architecture in a knowledgeable way, the references in Mr. Wickham's papers to the churchwardens accounts are light relief to strict architectural investigation and mystifying terminology. For instance: at Aughton, Dr. Plumbe, the Surgeon, was paid 2 guineas in 1773 'for treating the Aughton poor'. Mr. Wickham compares this with the parish doctor at Wallasey who, in 1693, got £2 for 'dressing and cleaning Catty Johnes her leg'. Whilst at Widdicombe, in Devonshire (adds Mr. Wickham), *c.* 1700, Dr. Ball got £8 'for curing Dorothy ffrench's leg and keeping the same sound from any more costs and charges'. Sadly, later (we are told) he had to return £4 'because he did not p'fect and continue the cure according to his promise'. The paper tells us that a gallery was erected in the church in 1735, for singers; and that 28s was spent on 43 dinners for Ann Monk, singer. In 1744, the Leverpule Singers got 2s, but the Rainford Singers, later, only 1s — so perhaps, even in those days, the 'Mersey' sound was in favour!

Church orchestras were in full swing (to use the Vicar's expression) in Lancashire churches, during the latter half of the 17th century; and at Aughton, in 1800, purchases of a 'hautboy', new bass viol, new bassoon, and clarinet were made. (Mr. Wickham employed orchestras in St. Andrew's Church on occasion, bringing the music of Mozart, Handel and other famous composers to his parishioners.)

Turning to 'Some Notes on Billinge', Canon Miller, Vicar of Billinge, and Mr. Wickham were great friends and had many a mutual discourse at one or other vicarage. Canon Miller, a bachelor of means, was exceptionally good to the Wickhams, and provided £50 a year towards Monica's medical training.

When Mr. Wickham left Wigan for Ampton, in 1916, Canon Miller wrote in the Billinge parish magazine . . . "By the departure . . . of the Rev. W. A. Wickham . . . Billinge loses the presence of a very old friend, who took a real interest in its welfare.

"We shall always have to thank him for his advice that Mr. (now Sir) T. G. Jackson, R.A., be asked to undertake the restoration of the church, a restoration of which Billinge is justly proud . . . again and again, he gave the Vicar most valuable advice; and he has written a delightful history of the church, under the modest title of 'Some Notes on Billinge', a copy of which is preserved among our parish papers.

"He was devoted to architecture, and was often consulted by his brother clergy, on the subject . . ."

Mr. Wickham's paper on Hindley Chappell was devoted to an analysis of the historical and architectural facts, and of the personalities involved, to determine the answer to the question 'Who built Hindley Chappell?' He says that, to many, it may seem of small importance. "But truth is never unimportant."

Two different conclusions had already been reached, and had been published in two different editions of the County History. He regarded it as important to ascertain the facts, since Hindley Non-Conformists of the day were saying 'The Non-Conformists built and endowed the chapel, and Churchmen are using it'.

Mr. Wickham dwelt at length on four good reasons to the contrary, including the improbability of Puritan chapel-building at that time, the orientation of the chapel, and the character and position of the then Rector of Wigan (later to become Bishop Bridgeman). His firm conclusion was that the Non-Conformists were wrong.

As with Aughton, Mr. Wickham interested himself in the records and found Hindley a veritable treasure-house, the Churchwardens' Accounts starting as early as 1757. He recalls the origin of 'Crying Seats' — pew places which were sold at public meetings by the Cryer (who, in this case, got 2d a time for his trouble). At Hindley, in 1805, £2 17s 8d had been paid for 1,592 sparrow heads. (An Act of Parliament in 1566 required churchwardens to be responsible for the destruction of vermin, in their parish. At Warnford, in Hampshire, they were paying 1s for a fox, 1d a dozen for sparrows heads, and 1s for a jackdaw's nest.) Still at Hindley, Thomas Ryecroft, the 'dog-whipper', received 2½d for a new whip and 2s 6d for a hat — so the

St. Andrew's stray dog, at the consecration service, was by no means a phenomenon.

Although referred to, there was no mention of payments to the 'Bobbers', whose duty it was to perambulate the aisles during the church service and, with their staffs, to tap on the head anyone seen to be 'nodding-off'.

As Mr. Wickham said, things had come to a pretty pass at Hindley by 1797, for it was decided that the Constable should attend regularly at chapel 'and assist to procure good order on the Lord's day'.

Hindley Chappell had its choir with accompaniment, too. By 1788, there were four reed instruments and a 'vilincelle', augmented on great occasions by 'fidelles', 'hautboys' (oboes), French horns and other instruments.

When Mr. Wickham investigated Cockersand chapter house, he found the original floor under 2½ feet of earth. Obtaining the permission of the owner (for it was on private land), he and his helper(s)? — unnamed — dug it out, to get to the base of the central pillar, so as to be able to describe it and to get details of the floor. They also dug a trench two feet or more wide, along the north-east side, to establish the presence of a 'bench-table'.

Cockersand (he tells us) was one of 25 polygonal chapter-houses in England and Wales, of which 15 had already been destroyed. Of those, remaining, only nine were as perfect as Cockersand which 'in some respects is almost unique'.

In his paper, he wrote of the unusual feature of the three carved heads among the 'foliage' carving on the central pillar. He compared them with the pillars in Lincoln chapter house, Salisbury chapter house, and the 'toothache' heads at Wells Cathedral, which were reminders of the toothache cures at the shrine of Bishop Bitton in the 13th century — offerings from which helped to build the transepts. Concluding his paper, Mr. Wickham made recommendations for the improvement of the condition of Cockersand chapter house, in the best interest of antiquarians. Subsequent to his investigations and the presentation of his paper, Cockersand was included in the list of monastic buildings declared of national importance, Mr. Wickham being advised of this by letter from the Office of Works (Department of Ancient Monuments and Historical Buildings).

In 'Some Notes on Chapter Houses', Mr. Wickham had emphasised their vital role. Taking Hooker's quotation 'Cathedrals are glasses wherein we see the face of antiquity', he added that 'No part of a cathedral reflected a clearer image of olden times than the chapter house, which was the building for the solemn assembly of the community for worship, deliberation, discipline and instruction.''

*A selection of Mr. Wickham's literary works.*

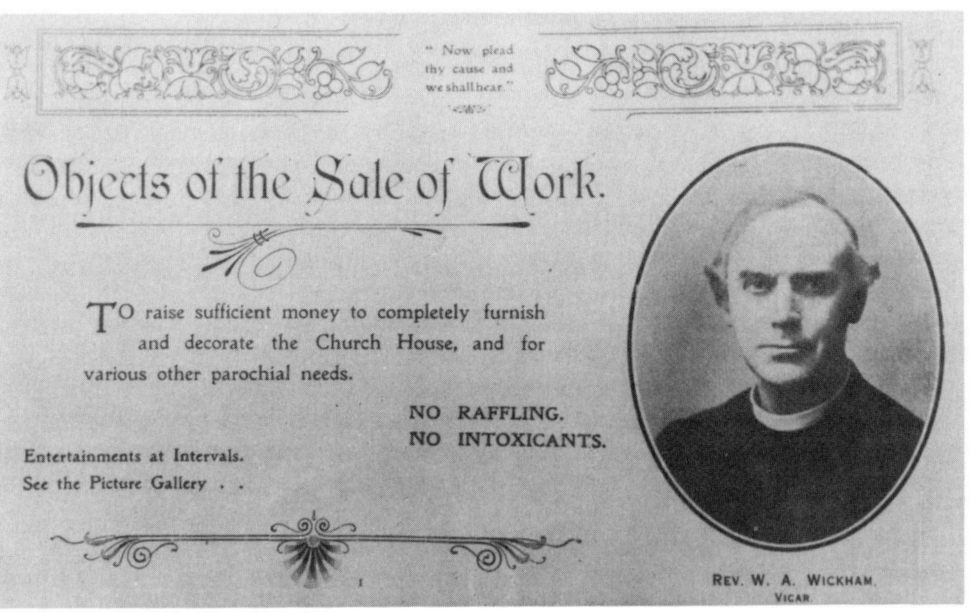


*Page from programme for a St. Andrew's sale of work.*

Cockersand had become a family burial-place, its internal structure and beauty disappearing under earth. Yet it was a national treasure, to be preserved. Mr. Wickham's heart must have been gladdened by the letter he received, giving official protection to Cockersand and the assurance of its future maintenance in good order.

By any standards, all this extra-parochial activity was a remarkable achievement. Mr. Wickham seems to have had the capability to reverse Parkinson's Law. For him, *time* expanded to fufil the work.

# Chapter 13



*WIGAN TO AMPTON*

Mr. Wickham was taken ill in January 1916, and was off duty for two months. Between February and August of that year (reading the parish magazine issues in retrospect), it is obvious that the Vicar knew that his days at St. Andrew's were numbered and that he must prepare his parishioners for a change.

There were little inserts about warnings from his doctor; a message of concern for him from the Bishop; and, lastly, a 'cri de coeur' that he (the Vicar) ''hopes to go on doing the work as well as he can, for as long as he can anyhow do it''.

He travelled a long way to recuperate, to Suffolk — and took Mrs. Wickham with him. Did any of his parishioners speculate as to an ulterior motive? In fact, a clergyman friend of his at Hoylake corresponded with a friend of *his,* the Rev. H. C. Dobrée, who had the living of Great and Little Livermere, the parish next to Ampton — and, through the latter, heard that the living of Ampton was becoming vacant. The Vicar and his wife went to Suffolk as the Rev. Dobrée's guests.

Ampton, in a quiet rural setting, with its population of 120 (25 houses, four alms-houses, and a post office) plus a wartime population increased by way of the 150-bed Red Cross hospital at Ampton Hall — must have seemed like God's gift to Mr. Wickham in his tired, run-down state of health.

The August issue of the parish magazine broke the news (just!) in a footnote: ''N.B. Just as we go to press, the Vicar has, with the permission of the Bishop of Liverpool, accepted the small Rectory of Ampton, near Bury St. Edmunds, in Suffolk; and hopes it may be possible for him to settle in there, early in October''.

On August 27th, Mr. Wickham announced from the pulpit the name of his successor.

The September magazine dealt fully with his impending departure, under the headings

IS THE VICAR GOING TO LEAVE ST. ANDREW'S?
WHEN IS HE LEAVING?
AS A RECTOR, WILL HE BE BETTER OFF?
(This in reply to friendly congratulations as to his 'betterment'.)

Mr. Wickham pointed out that his income would drop by one-third, adding, "No earthly master provides so well for his servants as does God, especially if they are content to leave matters to Him, and follow His guidance".

## WHAT SORT OF A PARISH IS THE VICAR GOING TO?

Here followed a comprehensive pen-sketch of Ampton. The village; the countryside around; the church and its rectors — one had been Henry Alford, composer of the favourite Harvest-tide hymn, 'Come, Ye Thankful People, Come'; Ampton Hall and its great historical personalities, which included Vice-Admiral Fitzroy, who commanded the 'Beagle' on Charles Darwin's epoch-making voyage; and, 'nailing his own colours to the mast', 'There is no public-house and no Dissenting-house of any kind'.

The Vicar rounded if off with the message, "Thus, a retiring-place has mercifully been provided...where there is much that is pleasant, and where he will find as much work as he can do well, without being over-burdened...Ampton...must not be a place to settle down in, but, rather, one for making more careful preparations for the final Exit...He asks his dear people of St. Andrew's to pray for him that his last years may be good ones." (He was now nearly 68.)

And, of his successor, he wrote..."He will come...with high hopes...See to it, dear people, that he is not disappointed...if my work amongst you has been *good* work, it will be made clear, now".

During the few months prior to the Vicar's leaving there had been great activity in the parish, in a quiet way, in view of Mr. Wickham's dislike of personal gifts.

Mr. James Lowe, people's warden, was the prime mover in this; and his suggestion that the Vicar's 38 years of ministry be commemorated *in* the church, in his lifetime, by the provision of a stained-glass memorial window, was heartily approved.

Abbott's of Lancaster were commissioned to design and make an East window on the theme of the Te Deum. Any excess money raised would be used to buy small family mementos. The idea was to present Mr. Wickham with a coloured drawing of the window at a leaving ceremony.; and to invite him back for the dedication.

On November 8th, a great gathering of congregation and friends took place at St. Andrew's Schools, the proceedings being reported

*'Dressed in their best.' Miners' women with 'snap' — baskets and tea-cans, 1891 outside St. Andrew's Church. (O.G.P.)*

'Pay-day crowd.' Amused by the photographer. Note young pit-workers with safety lamps, 1891. (L.S.)

'Pit-brow lasses.' Tipping tubs of coal into the screening chute, at Douglas Bank Colliery, 1891. (L.S.)

*'Loosening and "filling" coal, after blowing the face', 1891. (Damaged L.S.)*

*Wigan: 'Rag-and-bone man', 1891. (O.G.P.). Reveals long exposure problems (balloons waving about, and child movement).*

at length in the 'Wigan Examiner'. (Referring to the occasion in the December magazine issue, the Vicar commented, with a last touch of humour''...a very fair account...though it is scarcely necessary to say that the portrait which appeared at the head of it is not a good one. It might have been, if the Vicar had been at the Front, and had caught it from a bit of shrapnel''.)

Mr. Lowe, who 'chaired' the meeting, Mr. Haworth, Head of the St. Andrew's Schools, and Canon Matthew, Rector of Wigan, all paid generous tribute to Mr. Wickham's notable ministry. Mr. Haworth, who helped the Vicar with his lantern shows, told the audience how the Vicar had turned showman; and, speaking of all that had been raised from bare ground, in the parish and elsewhere (for Mr. Wickham's energies had also been responsible for the building of St. George's School, Wigan) said that he might well be called the Building Vicar. He also spoke of St. Andrew's Church, filled with memorials, through Mr. Wickham's initiative. Mr. Wickham was then presented with the coloured drawing of the memorial window, a carriage clock from churchwardens past and present, and a wallet containing 100 guineas. Presentations were also made to Mrs. Wickham and Miss Myrtle Wickham. So ended the last social event of his 38 years as Vicar of St. Andrew's, a few days after a similar gathering at Liverpool, when the Bishop presented him with a purse of 100 guineas in recognition of his varied, industrious, and successful labours for the Diocese and for the Cathedral.

The November issue of the parish magazine was devoted to a detailed account of the church and its furnishings, listing the various memorials, the donors, and the symbolism of the carvings and pictures. It also mentioned the inspiration for particular pieces, and indicated some 'Wickham-type' conversions. Even here, we glean more information on his travels and his influence upon people, for we learn that the altar linen came from the ladies of the Altar Linen Guild of St. Martin's, Scarborough. He had met some of them in Munich in 1881, whilst on his way to see the Oberammergau Passion Play. We also pick up an interesting link with his earliest-known photography, in that most of the figures on the reredos were copied from the altar screen in Winchester Cathedral. Other features of St. Andrew's church furnishings relate to known photographs taken by him. Was he the first clergyman ever to use photography in an organised way, as a tool of ecclesiastical craftsmanship? It is an interesting possibility.

The December issue of the parish magazine carried Mr. Wickham's farewell letter to his parishioners, detailing briefly the landmarks of his 38 years with them, and forming an expression of his personal 'balance-sheet'; much of this has been quoted elsewhere, in this book, but not "I have often reverently wondered why God, who helped me so wonderfully in other directions, willed that I should be single-handed when there was ample work for two priests".

After 12 months of work preparing the exhibition of his photographs, talking week by week with his three surviving daughters, meeting parishioners with recollections of him, working through all the St. Andrew's parish magazines from 1878 to 1916, and studying all other material that came into my hands, I asked myself the question 'Could *two* men, in the same situation, have achieved all that he achieved?'

I concluded that it was a combination of Mr. Wickham's great faith, great brain, great administrative skill, great driving force, and singled-minded objectivity; and his immense physical and spiritual energies which altogether sustained the momentum, over the critical years 1878—1910. It was the sheer magnitude of each major task, conceived and undertaken in single-handed leadership, which won him so may friends and staunch helpers, both in Wigan and far beyond it, as his competence and judgement in diverse ways were seen to be great and good.

Division of work with a Curate with the inevitable discussion and delegation, review, and re-assurance, yet still leaving Mr. Wickham with the final responsibility for the care of his people, must surely have dammed up the surging force of inspiration and initiative to some extent; and he did have the very active support of Mrs. Wickham, for many of those years. Also, devoted churchwardens and, it would seem, apart from some lean years, a band of helpers.

That the parish suffered in some ways, he was at pains to admit, in his farewell letter... "I have often left undone the things I ought to have done... [the story of all our lives] ...neglected my visits to the sick and the whole, neglected the due preparations of sermons, neglected the various opportunities for usefulness, and let 'busy idleness' interfere with hard work ..."

But, had he not committed these 'sins', would the schools have been built, with their lasting and large good, for instance? And, with so much of our national heritage destroyed, was not his 'busy idleness' at, say, Cockersand chapter house most worthwhile?

As he put it later in his last pastoral letter, referring to his ministry... "In so far as my work has been in the Lord, it cannot have been in vain. Beyond this, it is not possible to speak, for many of the results of my work can only be known to God".

The family left Wigan on November 22nd, 1916; and Mr. Wickham was instituted to the benefice of Ampton on the 28th. They moved into Ampton rectory on December 1st; life at Ampton had begun.

# Chapter 14



## *LIFE AT AMPTON*

Mr. Wickham's familiarity with Ampton is revealed in a notebook of his held (along with other 'Wickham' material) in Bury St. Edmunds Record Office. It contains extracts from Dutt's 'Suffolk', with corrections; details of the monumental brasses, with little sketches and side-notes about the kinds of head-dresses featured by the ladies of the brasses — fashion notes, you might say; descriptions of the Ampton church bells, with inscriptions and markings; expanded notes on Suffolk bell-founders; notes on Ampton and the Livermeres generally; and on Ampton's rectors and benefactors.

Ampton was more of an estate than a village, for almost all of its 800 acres was owned by the Squire of Ampton Hall and most of its inhabitants worked on the estate. According to the Rector, they lived in nice cottages, with gardens and plenty of roses. Some of them were people of many parts: the postmaster was also the parish clerk, estate carpenter and churchwarden.

There had been a Saxon church at Ampton, but all trace of it had gone, the existing church being mostly 15th century, with a small chantry on the north side, founded in 1478. Four brasses, dating from 1470 to 1790, were among the more interesting features of the church. The first-known rector was instituted in 1286, but, as the reference in the Domesday Book indicated, there must have been many more than the 54 recorded up to Mr. Wickham's incumbency.

With its long list of benefactors and parsons, it was an ecclesi-astical and ecclesiological goldmine to Mr. Wickham — and to others pursuing genealogical and similar interests with whom he correspon-ded. He himself added considerably to the genealogy of the Calthorpes (Calthrops) — a subject of research by a former rector, in 1905.

To Mr. Wickham's delight, the tenor bell tolled by him at his induction bore the name 'St. Andrew'; it was one of a ring of four, dating back to 1553 or earlier. He wrote to his old parishoners at

*Ampton Church: Henry Calthorpe memorial (erected by his widow, whose effigy also appears). Their ten children (including a 'chrysom' child), are shown on the monument. (Photo K. Ward.)*

*Ampton Church: Dorothy Calthorpe Memorial. She founded the alms-houses in Ampton; and her brother, James, the school. (Photo K. Ward.)*

Wigan of a good communicant roll; about 40 children at the Sunday afternoon service for them; and about 50 people at Evensong... "a very good church spirit in the place".

After Wigan, it was a very spartan life at Ampton rectory. Illumination was by paraffin lamp or candle; cooking was done on a three-burner paraffin stove; water was pumped up in the back kitchen from a spring that ran under the adjacent cemetery, so all water had to be boiled; rain water was collected for baths whenever possible; and, with coal extremely dear, wood was the main fuel for fires. There were frequent family excursions into the surrounding wooded countryside, by donkey-cart (hired at 3d a day) to gather wood; and, subsequently a great deal of sawing and log-chopping, which exercise Mr. Wickham much enjoyed.

The nearest shops were four miles away, at Bury St. Edmunds; and much shopping was done by bicycle, by those daughters at home. However, the rectory had a good vegetable garden, a strawberry patch, an asparagus bed, and a high wall of mellow brick which gave shelter and collected sun to support plums, peaches, apricots and a fig tree. The rectory, about 300 years old in parts, was half-thatched and had numerous small rooms, little low windows, and passages with obstacles for the head. It had a tall lilac hedge and lawn in front and, at the rear, a shrubbery-cum-copse and an old-world garden with extensive herbaceous borders. There was a constant battle with garden predators, notably bullfinches, pheasants, blackbirds and rats — keeping busy old Mr. Plummer, the jobbing gardener (nicknamed 'Colonel Dropper', by the Rector, on account of the perpetual 'dewdrop' on the end of his nose). All at home helped Mrs. Wickham, who had a busy time running the house with its primitive facilities. Although most pleasant in the warmer months, the rectory was very damp and cold in the winter; and frozen face-cloths on the washstands in the bedrooms (which the daughters recall) spoke silently of hardships to be endured.

1916 was a Happy Christmas for the Wickham family for Bernard, now a Bombing Officer to the 3rd (Reserve) Battalion, the South Staffordshire Regiment, was able to join them for part of the holiday; he had been to Buckingham Palace, to receive his Military Cross from King George V. Sadly, the spring of 1917 brought a shattering blow when they heard he had been killed in action near Ypres. He was only 22. The family gathered for a memorial service in Ampton church, as the register shows.

At the outbreak of war, Mr. G. A. Paley, owner of Ampton Hall, had at once put it at the disposal of the Suffolk Red Cross Society; it became their chief hospital and clearing station, with 150 beds and 50 staff. Mr. Wickham took over as C. of E. Chaplain which, as he said, "...adds a good deal to my work, and it also adds immensely to the interest...the men seem very glad to be visited...I go to each of the three wards for a service, every week, and also for Holy Communion as required".

The hospital closed on January 31st, 1919, having cared for 6,568 patients, of whom 40 died, 32 being buried in Ampton churchyard. Mr. Wickham was one of the moving spirits in establishing a permanent memorial to them in Ampton church. Eventually, panels on either side of the arch of the north chapel were used, for two memorials. One is a beautiful 'St. George' mosaic, put there by the Wickham family in memory of Bernard. The other is a similar mosaic, with a figure of St. Christopher, surmounted by a representation of the Red Cross; a panel on the north wall of the chantry lists the names of all who died at the Red Cross Hospital.

Mr. Wickham was also much involved in the establishment of a memorial at Ingham churchyard, where eight of the patients were buried. He designed the 2½ ton, 15th century style memorial, with its great cross of Portland stone and officiated at the special unveiling service, on November 22nd, 1919, following a similar service at Ampton Church.

He now had more time to spare and, although he had spoken of going to Ampton 'to lay down his bones', he began to apply his talents in various directions. He became a Sub-warden of the Central Society for Clerical Study; and a member of the local Clerical Society. He had also discovered that the most famous of Ampton's rectors had passed on, unrecognised; this was Jeremy Collier, M.A. (1679—?1685 incumbent), mentioned by Macaulay in his 'Essays' and 'History'. The Rector wrote an article about him, appealing for funds to raise a memorial in Ampton church; this appeared in the diocesan magazine, the money was raised and a memorial tablet was installed.

Later, he wrote a paper on 'The Parsons and Patrons of Ampton', which he read to the Suffolk Institute of Archaeology and Natural History. He also became a regular contributor to the diocesan magazine, under the pseudonym of 'Paganus', later sharing the responsibility for the 'Notes' section of the magazine with a colleague writing as 'Gashmu' (Canon L. Bird).

Mr. Wickham's copy of the 1905 edition of Dutt's 'Suffolk' soon began to be used extensively. First, he set to work on the Ampton entry, writing 'No', 'No', against the claim of 16th century and 17th century brasses; querying the re-opened priest's doorway; and correcting the name of the founder of the 1483 chantry. Then, he began to explore other churches in the area. Scraps of paper (from a pocket, no doubt) are stuck in against church monographs, each with delicate little sketches of architectural features, precisely labelled. An old envelope, re-addressed from Ampton to Sea View Cottage, Southwold (where the family occasionally holidayed) and post-marked October 16th, 1924, is covered with minute notes and sketches relating to Blythburgh church.

The envelope also bears a transportation time-table which enables Mr. Wickham's itinerary for the day to be traced (this in his 76th year). He travelled the four miles to Blythburgh on the narrow-gauge, single-track, Southwold—Halesworth railway. (Butt of many a joke, and subject of a series of comic postcards by a Reg Carter of South-wold. It was said that passengers even gathered groundsel for their canaries during unscheduled stops.)

To resume, Mr. Wickham obviously spent a considerable time in Blythburgh church. Dutt wrote ... "note the curious poppy-heads", in his monograph. Mr. Wickham added, 'Nave seats: 7 deadly sins'.

Then, Mr. Wickham walked the four miles to Dunwich, once believed to be the chief port on the Suffolk coast but, over the centuries, besieged by the sea. Dutt wrote of the ruins of All Saints Church and the Franciscan priory; Mr. Wickham amended the monograph to show that all had since gone into the sea, except for one buttress of All Saints, removed to a new site.

Having explored Dunwich, the Rector walked the four miles back to Blythburgh, and took the train back to Southwold: quite a day for a 75-year-old man with a 'tired heart'.

There were numerous references to 'Chrysom Children' (there was an effigy of a 'chrysom child' on the Calthorpe Memorial in Ampton church). The 'chrisom' was a child's white baptismal robe, used as a shroud, if it died within a month (becoming a 'chrysom child'). Mr. Wickham quotes "see First Book of Edward ... 'his white vesture, commonly called the crisome', p. 221; 'Hierugia Angicana', part II, p. 24[?]; 'Parish Registers' (Waters), 1687; Hampshire Registers (1649), p. 38[?].

Was ever a copy of Dutt's 'Suffolk' more extensively re-annotated and enlarged upon?

In 1922, the 'Bury [St. Edmunds] Post' published a series of articles written by Mr. Wickham dealing with Ampton benefactors and relating to the establishment of the Church of England boarding school and the almshouses in Ampton, by James and Dorothy Calthorpe, respectively.

James Calthorpe had established the trust in 1692, 'for six poor male children of the locality ...' The orders for the master and the boys were laid down in great detail — qualities, habits, manners, and behaviour, teaching (general and religious), complaints, curriculum, graces to be said, etc. Mr. Wickham's article covers, in great detail,

Buildwas. Chapter House
Interior

*Photography for
'Some notes on
Chapter Houses' (A.P.s)*

Wenlock. Wall Decoration'
in Chapter House

*Photography in the
West Country (A.P.s)*

112

the establishment, development and eventual decline of the school (due to agricultural depression during the late 19th century); then, its establishment as a public elementary school (with 41 pupils, when the article was written). It is a valuable contribution to the social history of Ampton. There was one incongruous section in the article by this strict teetotaller-clergyman. It was headed 'An Alcoholic Link'. Writing of the building of the school, Mr. Wickham mentioned that the contract required the trustees to give the carpenters "three comes of malt for their small beer in ye sd. works for ye due performance thereoff". He linked this with the building of the Duomo at Siena, when the clerk-in-works was allowed to give wine to the workmen, so far as he should think it" Pro melioramento ipsius operis" — the helping forward of the work; and he added "So little Ampton is joined by an alcoholic link with Italy".

Dorothy Calthorpe, who died in **1693**, gave money to endow an almshouse at Ampton for six poor widows or old maids of **60** years or older. They were to receive £6 a year for meat and drink (so that, with their own spinning, they might live comfortably); £4 a year for winter firing; a dark-coloured serge gown and petticoat every Easter Sunday (when they should all appear at the Communion); and any money left over to buy what they most needed. Mr. Wickham added that there had never been enough money from the endowment to maintain more than four inmates.

The Calthorpe memorials in Ampton church are beautifully executed; on Dorothy's is the inscription 'She made the poor her heirs'.

A final article by Mr. Wickham, titled 'The Bulldog', revealed him returning to his favourite theme, the place of the church schools in the national educational system. He appealed to Suffolk church-people to be bulldogs in the matter of the closure of the small village schools 'for administrative economies', urging them to hold on to them like grim death. From his inexhaustible store-house of references, he quoted from Miss H. C. O'Neill's 'Devonshire Idylls'. From the chapter on the 'School and its Scholars', he referred to the visit of the Inspector who scarcely knew the head from the tail of the village child ... "His report is neatly printed, and lies, one in a dusty heap of pamphlets, on the office shelves ... but the children are still alive ... and, as grown men and women, play their part, and help to make Devon what it is'.

Mr. Wickham's contention was that church and religion and social life generally would lose immensely if village schools were closed; they existed for something higher and better than mere scholarship — they were especially schools of character, with their definite church atmosphere, professedly religious resident teachers, and the influence of the parson. Writing of the various difficulties, he outspokenly expressed the view that the greatest was... "the disappointing attitude of many Churchmen — their failing hearts, their apathy, their close-fistedness... courage has her chance, when there are difficulties to be overcome".

In 1925, Beatrice Everett, of Ingham, went to work at Ampton rectory as daily maid/cook, Youngest of a family of six girls, of whom all but she were away in service as maids or cooks, the work fitted in with the responsibility of looking after her mother. Beatrice still lives where she was born; and the rambler growth from a cutting given to her by Mr. Wickham puts on a splendid show around the front door of her cottage each year. Among other things, she recalls the hectic task of keeping five fires going in the rectory for most of the year; taking over the cooking, so that the girls at home could go skating on frozen-over Livermere lake; and picking and boxing flowers from the garden for the Rector to send to Miss Myrtle.

Of Mr. Wickham she said, recently, "If ever there was a saint on earth, he was". In her time, Mr. Wickham periodically had to retire to bed for a few days, to rest his 'tired heart'. Then came a serious illness, and she did not see him for a few weeks. He eventually emerged, possessor of a luxuriant beard; and Beatrice did not recognise him until he greeted her. During his serious illnesses, Beatrice's mother used to share in the overnight 'sitting up' duties. Mr. Wickham would say to her, "Mrs. Everett, you are just the one I need; you are so quiet, but I know you are there".

In November 1926 the Rector suffered another blow; his beloved wife was taken ill and died of pneumonia. Grief-stricken though he was, although one of his friends took the Funeral Service, he himself took the Committal; later, he entered it into the register, making a marginal note that there was room for one more in the grave.

At Ampton, as at Wigan, the registers were kept meticulously. Service by service, one knew how many were in the congregation (in Red Cross hospital days there was a 'breakdown' also into patients, nurses, and the Matron). The *number* of coins in the offertory was given (presumably to provide an average); weather was recorded; and, on one occasion (when the owners of Ampton Hall, opposite the church, were Roman Catholics and not averse to games on Sunday), a note of a cricket match which started during Matins and was still in progress at Evensong.

Nothing was too much trouble for him. He pasted this note into the register, against the entry of the burial of Alfred Trudgett on June 27th 1923.

"Note. Alfred Trudgett had lived in Ampton for 40 years, leaving it a few years ago... I have promised his wife interment with her husband, if she should die while I am Rector of Ampton. The grave was dug deep enough to allow this..." Mrs. Trudgett outlived the Rector, but the promise was kept.

After the death of Mrs. Wickham, Cicely and Caroline stayed at home to look after their father; Cicely was now the church organist and also the parish clerk. Mr. Wickham was showing his years and his mobility was reduced. However, he coped with the parish and continued his journalism. He was writing for the February 1929 issue of the diocesan magazine; and was answering criticisms in the March issue.

Then, on April 7th, 1929, the church register records 'Low Sunday. No Services — Rector down with pneumonia'.

He never recovered, although he kept up his writing, from his bed, almost to the end — and added his little statistics to the service register. He collapsed on May 27th; and, in the register, we read:

May 30th. The Rector, William Arthur Wickham, died — 6.0 a.m.
R.I.P.

Seventeen years earlier, he had indicated his wishes in connection with his eventual death, in the form of a cutting from The 'Times' obituary column. "No biography, no flowers or funeral show, possibly a few wild flowers scattered over my grave. Funeral as little mournful as possible.

"The earthly end of a poor sinner, who died thankful to God for a long and very happy life."

He was buried in his wife's grave, in the little churchyard of St. Peter's, Ampton, on a sunny Saturday afternoon — in a simple medieval-shaped coffin of unpolished elm. The only floral tributes were those from people's gardens. At the close of the service, a peal was rung on the bells.

The 'Bury [St. Edmunds] Post' said of his writings in the diocesan magazine, "All who read his articles will agree that they displayed to the full his erudition and his abiding sense of humour. His learning never showed a heavy touch, but none-the-less it was unmistakable in all his writings."

The news of Mr. Wickham's death was heard at Wigan with deep sadness and a special funeral service was held at St. Andrew's Church, to coincide with the service at Ampton. Mr. Wickham's old Billinge friend, Canon Miller, helped to officiate.

On the following day, there was a memorial service in St. Andrew's Church. In the course of it the Vicar, the Rev. J. M. Buckmaster, B.A., said of Mr. Wickham "[he] ...had a great deal to put up with. He was attacked for all sorts of things, he was attacked most scurrilously, in the local Press...Mr. Wickham had a sense of humour. He cut out all the articles and placed them in a scrap-book, to be preserved.

"Mr. Wickham had no Degree. He never had a chance to go to University. Had he done so, he would have come out on top. Whatever he gave his mind to, he mastered it... he never desired honours, and did not seek them... he was not a man of compromise... there was something of the Puritan about Arthur Wickham.

"He never had prizes in the Sunday School in the parish. If he lost some of the children, it did not matter; he was there to teach the faith... the Church spoke for him."

Mr. Wickham's old friend and School Headmaster at St. Andrew's wrote an appreciation for the parish magazine (from which I have quoted, elsewhere). And, in the same issue, the Rev. J. M. Buckmaster wrote, "What we in St. Andrew's owe under God to William Arthur Wickham, it is impossible to state in words... we mourn his loss, but we rejoice in what God enabled him to do".

In 1979, 50 years after Mr. Wickham's death, one of his former St. Andrew's choirboys wrote to me, "I feel sure that my own life has benefited from the leavening influence of this kind-hearted and well-disciplined Victorian".

The July 1929 issue of the diocesan magazine for the county of Suffolk was very much a 'William Arthur Wickham' issue. The Bishop, in his letter, wrote, "It is with widespread sorrow that the readers of our magazine will have heard of the death of the Rev. W. A. Wickham who, over the signature of 'Paganus', has many a time contributed notes to our pages, written with a quiet humour and a manifest delight in his ministry that must often have brought cheer to the heart of some tired or worn brother incumbent. His service well fulfilled, to him has come the 'Well done'; he has entered in to the joy of the Lord."

Julian G. Tuck, Rector of Tostock and writer of the 'In Memoriam' notice was a contemporary of Mr. Wickham's at Lichfield Theological College and was present at his ordination. He praised the high moral standard Mr. Wickham had set himself, from the first, and maintained throughout his life. Writing of Mr. Wickham's talents, he mentioned that, when the 'Life and Episcopate of G. A. Selwyn, D.D.' was being written, Mr. Wickham's help was sought and some pages contributed by him. And his great friend of Ampton days, 'Gashmu' (Canon L. Bird) wrote, "Wickham of Ampton recalled to the mind Bacon's words about reading maketh a full man. His contributions reminded me often of an old two-volume anthology called (I think) 'Books and Days', in which one came across queer and forgotten lore.

"And to what he had gathered from many authors, were added

all the varied experiences of his own 80 years of pilgrimage . . . of all the long line of Rectors of Ampton, I doubt if any loved each several stone of the little church more than he . . .''

. . . 'Eros unarm,
The long day's task is done, and we must rest.'

[This quotation puzzled the author, but the 'New Larousse Encyclopaedia of Mythology' provided the answer. Here, Eros is called the one 'Who brings harmony to chaos', the co-ordinator of the elements.

How well it fitted Mr. Wickham's great talents for creating and organising!]

Then followed Mr. Wickham's last article, written the year before and dealing with the liberty given to use extempore prayer in the 1928 Prayer Book, but held over ''in view of the accident to the Book'' (Mr. Wickham's quotation).

It was a very substantial article, occupying 5 of the 18 pages of the diocesan magazine and quite beyond the writer's competence to assess. But he did make the point that ''The more one thinks of it, the more it seems to open 'a wide door and effectual' for good or evil''. And, towards the end, he quotes Dr. South . . . 'Can there be any sense of propriety in beginning a new, tedious prayer in the pulpit just after the church has, for nearly an hour together . . . been praying for all that can possibly be fit for Christians to pray for'.

Mr. Wickham was not against extempore prayer, made use of it, and said so, in his article; he was for brevity and objectivity. What he appeared to fear was that too many people might have to suffer listening too long to *preachers,* rather than to the *Church.* One senses that he was thinking back to his own long experience, conscious of the fact that there was just not enough time in the world to accomplish all that needed to be done; and that time should not be wasted in needless preaching and unproductive listening.

Of Mr. Wickham's own preaching, we have no record, but we do have an address he delivered to his fellow-clergymen of the Wigan and District Clergy Union, at Billinge parish church, on April 30th, 1907; an address subsequently printed for distribution to the members.

It falls into two parts, the first of which is the basic platform of the address; and the second the application to the clergy in their life and work.

Mr. Wickham makes this opening statement. ''There are two great facts, which we have to bear in mind as we go through life.

1.   That we are so made that we cannot be satisfied here.
2.   That it is our duty and our wisdom to be contented.''

These facts are enlarged upon, drawing from many sources, biblical, literary, and even musical, for his inspiration. Put at its simplest, it is the cultivation of contentment in this life, through faith. Our place is where God has put us — and there we should stay, not shirking our personal cross, until God sees fit to move us.

Mr. Wickham: "If a man can but firmly believe that God knows where he is, and keeps him there, as he at first put him there...he will soon be able to learn the secret...to be content...We must try to be content, because discontent makes us unhappy, and also because it hinders our work...if no fresh call comes to us, God is constantly telling us to stay where we are."

Mr. Wickham spoke to 'his brethren' of the dangers of discontent through tiredness, uncongenial work, ambition; and of clergyman who "like butterflies or angels, passed from parish to parish accumulating a study-full of Testimonials of Love and Respect, but who stayed scarcely long enough in one place to meet with real difficulties, let alone understand them".

His message, then, is: "...take [circumstances] as they are, and make the best of them. Those who have done great things are not men who repined that they were born in another place or age, but those who did their work from day to day...."

"And even suppose old age comes to us, or failing health, or waning power, what then? Still the word must be 'work on, do your best, and be content...until the Hand that moved thee into thy place, move thee away from it'."

He concluded: "So let each one of us 'abide with God', wherever we are called by Him to work...in calm content".

If the above was hard to accept, in poor St. Andrew's parish, from the Sunday pulpit, at least his parishioners knew that, for Mr. Wickham, it did not mean waiting for God to do something about bad housing, lack of schools, typhoid epidemics, adult illiteracy, primitive sanitation, poverty — and many other social problems.

For, during the week, Mr. Wickham, his wife, and their band of devoted helpers strove to lighten the burden of their parishioners individual crosses, to relieve the worst of their anxieties; and, through their works and a constant promise of help in time of trouble, to create a slightly better environment in which a tiny seed of contentment could grow, in faith.

## ...AND BACK TO WIGAN

In October 1918, the Bishop of Liverpool dedicated the Wickham memorial window, in St. Andrew's Church, Wigan. In his address, Dr. Francis Chavasse spoke of the great joy it had given him to be there to unveil the window and the memorial. Reminding the congregation of the inscription on the monument to Sir Christopher Wren, in St. Paul's Cathedral, he said, "If you need a memorial to the work of William Wickham, look around this beautiful church, which was adorned and beautified through him, with wonderful skill and taste and love".

They had done rightly in seeking in that window to add yet another memorial to his work. But they could give him a yet higher and greater memorial still — the testimony of their own lives, that "the ministry he had served amongst them had been fruitful of good ..."

It is most appropriate that the man who was not only his Bishop and co-worker in the cause of the new Liverpool Cathedral, but also a close family and personal friend, should pronounce the final words of praise and thanksgiving for the life and work of William Arthur Wickham, a truly remarkable Victorian gentleman.